ACTIVE ACTING

Exercises and Improvisations Leading to Performance

By Leslie Abbott
Diablo Valley College

PUBLISHING COMPANY
P.O. Box 68
Belmont, California 94002
(415) 591-3505

Consulting editor: Dr. Elio Zappulla

Cover illustration and graphics by Debora Zink

Printed in the United States of America

ISBN: 0-89863-114-9

CONTENTS

PREFACE v

CHAPTER 1
DEVELOPING CREATIVITY 1

CHAPTER 2
DEVELOPING RELAXATION AND FREEDOM 17

CHAPTER 3
TOOLS OF ACTING 31

CHAPTER 4
CHEKOVIANS 49

CHAPTER 5
IMPROVISATIONS 57
FIRST CHARACTER 81
SECOND CHARACTER 95
THIRD CHARACTER 109
FOURTH CHARACTER 110

CHAPTER 6
DEVELOPING YOUR CHARACTERIZATION 115

CHAPTER 7
THE ENCOUNTER SESSION 125

PREFACE

A little more than fifty years ago Constantin Stanislavsky, the co-founder of the Moscow Art Theatre, formulated a series of acting principles that came to be known throughout the world as the Stanislavsky System. In the United States this system found its most articulate spokesmen in some of the members of the celebrated acting company, the Group Theatre. With considerable variations such people as Harold Clurman, Lee Strasberg, Stella Adler, Elia Kazan, and Robert Lewis became the major interpreters of the "method," the popular American descriptive title for the acting principles set down by Stanislavsky.

Two Russians who settled in the United States, Michael Chekhov and Richard Boleslavsky, assisted greatly in communicating Stanislavsky's precepts. In addition to teaching and directing, these two men left invaluable texts that have been a major influence on every acting book that has appeared in the English-speaking world. Boleslavsky's small but invaluable book, *Acting: The First Six Lessons*, dealt with six tools of acting: Concentration, Observation, Memory of Emotion (Affective Memory), Sense Memory, Characterization, and Rhythm. Chekhov's "To the Actor" was most helpful in illuminating Stanislavsky's concepts of "physicalizing the action" and the idea that all movement stems from a center of energy within the character that the actor is playing.

Reduced to its essentials, the "method's" emphasis is on truth, in making everything the actor does in a performance believable to himself and therefore to the audience. This emphasis on truth is at the heart of all successful, effective acting and is necessary if the actor is to create a character in whom the audience can believe.

While the Stanislavsky System remains at the center of any good actor's craft, the development of many psychological theories since then has altered our perception of human behavior and expanded our knowledge of how creativity can be nurtured. It is these psychological theories, combined with the teachings of Stanislavsky, that are explored in ACTIVE ACTING, EXERCISES AND IMPROVISATIONS LEADING TO PERFORMANCE.

ACTIVE ACTING is designed to provide beginning and intermediate acting students with a series of exercises, joined with creative and character analyses that are a practical step-by-step working program for learning how to act. These exercises will lead you to understand how "method" theories are translated into practice. The exercises are designed to give you the freedom to use your emotional and sensory resources without censorship, to learn how to trust your intuitive processes, to learn to trust your acting partners, to make an emotional commitment appropriate to the character, and to surrender to the pursuance of your character's objectives. The sequence of exercises is designed so that the work becomes increasingly complicated and demands more emotional commitment on the part of the actor. All the exercises in ACTIVE ACTING involve the specific use of one or more of the six tools of acting, and each of the exercises specifies which tools must be used in the exercise if it is to be successful. Once you have begun to understand how to use these tools effectively, you are on your way to becoming a good actor.

During the first semester you will want to work on the exercises and material covered in the first six chapters, augmented by scene work using the chapter on "Developing Your Characterization" as a guideline. Starting with chapter seven, the exercises are designed for your second or third semester acting classes and should be utilized in connection with scene work. Reviewing the chapter on "Developing Your Characterization" and answering in detail the characterization questionnaire before doing your scene work are important in developing your acting skills.

ACTIVE ACTING is designed so that *you will learn* by *doing.* Most books on acting are based on the theories of Stanislavsky, but these books rarely give practical exercises that translate these theories into practice. ACTIVE ACTING does not dwell on these theories but embraces their intentions through many kinds of improvisational exercises which lead you to practical application of these theories in performance. By the time you have completed all the exercises in this book you may not be a polished actor, but you will have many of the basic tools that will allow you to work as a creative performing artist. As with all art, acting is a process of maturation and hopefully you will continue to develop and grow as an artist.

CHAPTER 1

DEVELOPING CREATIVITY

Every actor's creativity can be improved. The notion that artists are born either creative or not creative, and that this quality is thereby immutable should be rejected. Creativity, like many other human psychological traits, is benefited by training experiences. Thus all of our theories and exercises to expand creativity included in this book apply to all actors regardless of their present talent.

Creativity is the core of the acting process. As such, it is a vitally important ability to explore because it is so poorly understood and developed in acting sessions and because its nourishment can lead to a far richer, more satisfying, and more productive performance.

For the actor, "creativity" means an approach to life situations characterized as unusual, satisfying, and productive. Creative acting is marked by its novelty and its illumination of human behavior in an acute, perceptive way. An actor's creativity is sometimes embodied in his ability to combine remote associations and divergent thinking into an artistic entity.

What do we mean by remote associations? It refers to the creative act of relating two well-known phenomena that are not ordinarily associated. In literature we read, "Life's but a walking shadow" or "Now is the winter of our discontent." In both cases the individual elements are familiar, but the aesthetic satisfaction comes through the author's sensitivity to the relation between these remote elements. An actor may recognize the not-so-remote association between a horse's eating habits and a character's table manners. In playing the gulled husband in TARTUFFE, the actor may recognize that the character struts like a peacock.

Divergent thinking, which can enhance creativity, refers to thinking that leads to many ways of developing a character. It might include observing animals whose mannerisms can be matched to characterizations, recognizing an unusual physical manifestation in a person that betrays that person's inner psyche, listening not to the words a person speaks but to the tonal quality of one's words which may suggest a feeling contrary to the one the person is trying to convey. It might be expressed by an actor who as a character is engaged in learning a new dance step while simultaneously plotting a murder.

Let's examine the phases of the creative process. Understanding these phases can be helpful in considering the specific activities that will aid in developing your creativity as an actor.

These stages of the creative process are by no means definitive. They overlap and do not necessarily follow a set sequence. Different people use different terminology to describe these elements of the creative process; the important thing is to recognize that the phenomena are essential to the creative process.

Briefly, creative acting involves these four aspects:

ACQUISITION. Before you as an actor are able to relate various elements of your experience in unusual, productive, and satisfying ways, you must be open to experience, able to perceive and sense your environment, and be aware of your own internal feelings.

ASSOCIATION. You must be able to take the experiential elements that you have acquired, relate them to each other, and be capable of associating two or more experiences which can lead to an illuminating performance when they are associated.

EXPRESSION. Once these elements are connected, they must be expressed in vocal and bodily expressive form. This implies that the vocal and physical apparatus must he technically developed so that the association can be communicated in a satisfactory way.

SELECTIVITY. Many elements can be generated in the course of a rehearsal that are creative, but the selection of those elements that satisfy the situation and rejection of those that are worthless is essential. This selectivity distinguishes the bizarre from the creative and the meaningful from the mundane.

ACQUISITION

Acquiring knowledge and experience provides the actor with some materials to work with in order to be creative. You must have information and experiences that have been felt and integrated into your being. Since it is impossible for an actor to experience everything at first hand, you must read novels and biographies so that you may develop insight into human behavior that is different from your own. Although this is vicarious experiencing, it will help you come to understand why people behave in ways contrary to your own responses. Moreover, you must develop a sympathetic understanding of this human behavior that is foreign to your own. As an actor, you must become tuned to hearing the sounds of nature and man. You must see the design, the spatial relationships of man and his environment, if you are to become an accurate portrayer of human nature. Occasionally we see a successful actor without formal training, but it seems safe to say that knowledge increases the probability of a creative and successful performance.

The ability to learn is a prerequisite for the acquisition of information, but there is a different requirement for the acquisition of experiences. Creativity can be enhanced by an increased sensitivity to both direct and vicarious experience. Developing your senses to increase awareness of your environment greatly enhances the resources with which you can create. Such development of the senses includes:

1. Becoming sensitive to tactile relating possibilities both in terms of other people and inanimate objects. Is the furniture pleasant to the touch? Do you want to touch other people? Do you enjoy doing so?
2. Recognizing temperature, climate, weather, circumstances, and the way they condition an individual's response to a moment. Is it so hot that tempers flare, or is it so cold that you feel sullen and withdrawn?
3. Becoming aware of how color and spatial relations influence an individual's temperament and emotional attitudes. Are your surroundings pleasant to the eye? Do you feel cramped in close quarters or lost in large spaces?
4. Learning that external rhythm imposed on an individual will color that person's emotional responses. Does the clickety-clack of the train wheels on the track makes you feel lonely, or is it speeding you home? Does the clanging of the assembly line

jangle every nerve in your body? Becoming aware of how your senses respond to stimuli in a given situation enhances the possibility of giving an effective performance.

Acquiring knowledge and developing the senses without developing feelings and emotions that allow experiences to be felt and integrated into the self will result in your not being able to give a satisfactory performance. Emotional blocks may restrict your ability to perceive and learn. Many childhood experiences prevent a person from being able to obtain the necessary emotional freedom essential to acting. Unresolved emotional problems may block off or distort perception and blunt the ability to sense experiences accurately as, for instance, when fear of criticism makes an actor hear critical words where none exist. It is interesting to note that, in giving an actor a critique including ten statements of which eight are complimentary and two are non-complimentary, it is frequently true that the actor hears only the adverse comments. Both under-reacting and over-reacting to a given situation on the part of an actor is usually tied to complex emotional problems; often we observe actors who cannot allow themselves to feel or project deep affection for others in a performance since in life their fear of rejection is too great.

It is regrettable too that some actors find it easier to project hostility than to project love and humanism. If you have such inhibitions they will diffuse and distort your ability to assimilate new ideas, experience and understand different forms of human behavior than your own, and will distort your perception of your own being. Actors with such emotional blocks find their openness to experience seriously curtailed and their repertoire of resources to employ in their acting sharply diminished. The exercises and theories expressed in this book are intended to remove such emotional blocks. In the exercises it is imperative that you establish and maintain an atmosphere of honest and open communication. Whether working on structured scenes or various kinds of improvisational exercises, you should endeavor to accept a position of vulnerability and not fear exposure of both your strengths and weaknesses as a human being. From these acting sessions you and your fellow actors should develop a more profound and realistic picture of what individual people, human interaction, and you yourselves are like.

ASSOCIATION

Taking experiential elements and associating and combining them in new ways constitutes an essential part of the creative process. The combination of corned beef and cabbage was a happy one for the hearty eater. The recognition that the development of the fetus from conception to birth is paralleled in the life cycle from birth to death advanced our knowledge of both prenatal existence and of life itself. In both cases, the creative act involved using elements already in the creator's experience and realizing that relating them would lead to something new and desirable.

Association can occur with information, sensations, or feelings. All are very important for creativity. As an example, the fetus and the life cycle of man is an association of information. The evolving of the fetus can be equated to the ages of man, and one can see that the behavior of one is parallel to the behavior of the other. Psychotherapy recognizes that many dreams and free associations are related because they elicit similar feelings. The symbol of a bird of prey represents an exploitative person. A person in their dreams frequently feels that they are the victim of a bird of prey—about to be pounced upon and that they are helpless. Associations can occur in many ways; the more highly developed your ability to associate in all ways, the greater your possibilities for making unusual and satisfying connections of elements that are not obviously related.

Unfortunately, many actors have unconscious blocks that inhibit their ability to associate. In acting exercises we frequently encounter an actor's fear of letting their mind go uncontrolled and doing and saying anything that occurs organically because of the feeling that there is something in the unconscious that is frightening; such an actor is certain they will reveal deficiencies of personality and psyche that will make them vulnerable and subject to ridicule. This actor, consequently, cannot allow the freedom of associations but must keep them logical and controlled. The restriction of the ability to allow yourself to explore relations among various experiential elements can seriously limit your creativity.

While Constantin Stanislavsky, co-founder of the Moscow Art Theatre and the formulator of that acting process called the "method" in America, probably was never aware of the psychotherapy developed by Sigmund Freud; his acting theories embrace the Freudian technique of reporting a free train of thought without censorship or evaluation. This method should be applied to your acting with valuable results. The assumption in free association is that the thoughts that come to mind have a sequential connection to each other, although you may not see the connection immediately. Much of the value of improvisation as an actor's exercise lies in its power to concretely reveal to the performer the value of free association and the use of oneself without censorship or control of the psyche. For example, if you have been having a characterization problem the director may tell you, "Just do anything that comes into your head, no matter how silly or foolish it seems. Do it regardless of how you think observers will react!" By following and trusting this working method, you can very often arrive at the way the scene should be played. This approach is termed "working organically."

Learning how to associate remote elements can be developed by encouraging analogy. Describing a character as "cold as an iceberg" is a shorthand way of revealing to an actor some aspects of a person's personality. From it we gather that the person is austere, that much of the person's feelings are submerged and hidden, that the person has a potential for being dangerous to others.

Often we will discover actors who do not seem to perceive the obvious in terms of characterization. You must guard against not recognizing and acknowledging the true feelings essential to a portrayal should you have a strong defensive need to deny such internal feelings. For some actors this blocking takes the form of acting in opposition to their true feelings. For example, you might need to portray hostile feelings toward another person; but guilt, fear, or other motives may prevent your expression or even acknowledgement of this feeling. You may find it difficult to take any aggressive action and unconsciously equate natural, constructive assertiveness with cruelty and a lack of humanity. Since it is natural for all people to possess both constructive and destructive elements within their psyche, a technique that sometimes can help you to acknowledge these feelings is to "Act as if you felt just the opposite of the way you really do." If this technique releases you, then you will be better able to recognize your own emotional resources and employ them.

EXPRESSION

A creative act for an actor must be expressed through the use of his voice, his face, and his body. For a performing artist the emphasis in the art is in the form in which discoveries are expressed. When Martha Graham danced, the artistry was at least as largely important in the superb movement of her body as in the content and its uniqueness in her themes. In film, television, or the theater, the initial artistic creativity is that of the writer and it is incumbent on the actor to interpret that art in an illuminating and creative way. Consequently, learning how to move well, developing the resonance and range of one's voice, and possibly singing and dancing are all part of expanding one's ability to be a fine actor. Further, the development of skill in the use of expressing feelings in a symbolic way can be important. We get obvious examples of this in classical theater and in the Oriental theater.

On a less obvious plane, such symbolism is employed in the more realistic performing arts of the occidental world. This is one of the reasons why actors sometimes are asked to work with "animal images" whereby they portray various animals. We immediately conjure up a picture of a certain kind of person when we hear the expression "He eats like a horse." The unconscious factors that cause inhibitions are often due to cultural or interpersonal censure. The belief that ballet dancing is not masculine, or singing is uncouth, or artists are irresponsible, or actresses are immoral are all factors that may operate both consciously and unconsciously to inhibit the full expression of feelings in these areas. Many actors unconsciously do not approve of their desire to perform. They concurrently both want to succeed and not succeed as performers.

The atmosphere during acting sessions has a great deal to do with your developing creative freedom. If a congenial atmosphere can be established in which all the actors are mutually exploring means of obtaining creative freedom and everyone supports the creative efforts of each other, amazing progress can be made. It is important to work in an atmosphere in which only constructive criticism can prevail. In a constructive atmosphere you can give yourself permission to fail.

What this means simply is that neither you nor your colleagues impose upon you any premature, presumptuous value judgments while you are exploring the possibilities of either a role or exercise. You can feel free to expose your tender inner life. Usually most actors are delighted to see one another succeed; consequently, you need not be afraid to be vulnerable. Your inner life and your freedom to allow it to be exposed is likely to be the most important resources you have as an actor. If actors working together indulge in criticism, it automatically limits creative expression. In the early stages of training, I think it best if there is no discussion at all. Imaginative, creative work is rarely helped by discussion and, in the early stages of an actor's development, frequently is a drawback to the creative and imaginative processes. A portion of maintaining a positive atmosphere lies with the director-teacher; he/she may find it difficult to tolerate great creativity and unconsciously becomes defensive. It is important for the director to accept the notion that it is his responsibility to develop artists who are better than himself. The director-teacher must accept and not find damaging to his ego the fact that his actors will become better performing artists than him.

SELECTIVITY

Experiential elements that have been acquired, associated in various ways, and given means of expression may not of themselves result in a fine performance. For a performance to be creative, rather than merely bizarre, it must be evaluated as to its relevance to the situation and the specific work of art. Introducing psychedelic devices into high comedy, a slapstick performance into a tragedy, or a hyperactive performance into a Greek drama are all unusual connections between diverse elements, but their dramatic value in respect to their material is somewhat doubtful. In this sense, actors must ask themselves whether they are combining these elements harmoniously.

It is difficult to evaluate artistic excellence since it seems ephemeral, depending on the artist's own feelings about his work, the audience's reaction to his work, and the prevailing social trends. Being on the crest of a popular movement can be instrumental in making a successful acting career. The waxing and waning in popularity in any number of actors, including those who are truly talented as well as interesting personalities, illustrates the difficulty of the problem in evaluating an artistic achievement.

An actor's evaluation of his own work and, hence, selectivity of what he employs in a performance must be mostly intuitive. Still, there are some questions you can ask yourself:

1. Is my characterization truthful?
2. Is my characterization consistent? That is, does this person I am portraying always have a behavior pattern that can be justified in terms of the character's psychological makeup? You may have a good or bad "feeling" about some of the things you are doing. If so, perhaps you need to select other elements in creating your character and discard some of the elements you have been using. As you become more experienced, you will develop a degree of

objectivity about your work that will help you sense that something is wrong in your characterization and allow you to take steps to correct it.

Frequently the "unconscious" has advance information about the adequacy of elements used in a performance and signals this intelligence to you through bodily sensations. For example, some physical action you are making will not feel comfortable. Your ability to respond to these sensations can be very profitable in abandoning some traits and pursuing others. Of course there may be errors; but very likely, responding to your bodily sensations will be profitable since you utilize more of your bodily functions. Sometimes actors call this the "intuitive process"; it should be trusted.

Emotional blocks to adequate evaluation occur around the problem of decision-making. There are a number of reasons why a person may make incorrect selections. The choices of what to utilize in a performance may be distorted for many reasons:

1. You may have a fear of disappointing others or yourself.
2. You may have a general insecurity about your own competence.
3. You may have a compulsive perfectionism that distorts your ability to make correct selections or to properly evaluate your own performance.
4. You may have a wish-fulfillment need, a drive for achievement or competitiveness that can result in an unwarranted acceptance of your acting without sufficient self-criticism.
5. You may have a need to control spontaneity out of fear that your spontaneous reactions will be in conflict with your notions of morality, compassion, religious convictions, and proper social behavior.

Conflict, vacillation, or premature decisions can result. Frequently, a potentially fine actor will demand to be seen in performance before he is ready. The resulting premature performance may delay, by months, his ultimate success. To the degree that these factors are present, an actor must have difficulty choosing what elements to employ in a performance. In evaluating their own work, such an actor will tend either to accept their own choices uncritically or to reject worthwhile contributions. In either case, creative acting is not possible.

In evaluating and selecting what elements to use in a performance, you must concern yourself with the bodily feelings of "right" and "wrong." Children often trust these feelings so that, if they are uncertain about a course of action, they can depend upon their feelings about it—not that these feelings are invariably right. Unfortunately, adult actors tend to distrust these intuitive feelings. Developing an awareness of their existence will allow these feelings to be noticed and evaluated. One actor may find that his "feels" turn out to be valuable all the time, another may find them useful only in certain areas, while a third may learn to use other cues in conjunction with these "feels."

PERSEVERANCE

Creative ideas usually come frequently to the reasonably talented actor, but an attitude of perseverance is essential. The creative performance requires constant exploration; embryonic ideas may be brought to maturity and then either employed or rejected; the characterization must be "lived with" so that it can be thoroughly worked through. Some people feel that a performance should stand as it was spontaneously developed. For most actors this does not hold; a characterization most often conveys the feelings meant by the playwright. Furthermore, the actor must realize that the development of the creative process is not constant in a series of evenly spaced achievements. Actors will reach plateaus where their creativity will not seem to grow and where they seem to be caught in a period of employing only those processes which they have already discovered. At such times it is imperative for the actor to persevere until the actor achieves new creative insight.

The quality of one's perseverance must always be questioned. It is possible that an actor may stick to an idea, a characterization, beyond the point when it is fruitful. Conversely, an actor may give up an idea too quickly before the actor has explored all the possibilities and range inherent in the idea. Flexibility should be a guiding principle for the creative actor. The problem then is to avoid going from one idea to another without exploring the possibilities fully and also to avoid staying with one approach to a characterization far beyond the point where it is clear that it will not develop into anything of value.

In creating a role, you must guard against a falling off of your interest once the initial key to your characterization has been discovered. The rehearsal period is at least part drudgery and unrewarding; yet it is valuable since it can be utilized to refine and illuminate your initial creative discoveries. Sometimes an actor will fail to follow through in his creativity since the actor has ambivalent feelings toward authority. To act creatively may have the meaning, "I can do something better than the producer/director (authorities)." Because such actors have not resolved their authority feelings, this implication is much too threatening and prohibits them from carrying their portrayal through to perfection.

Actors will sometimes persevere in an idea beyond its usefulness for a variety of reasons. In this case, authority may again be a deterrent, but in a different way. For some actors, who are rebelling against authority, a non-creative or conforming act symbolizes submitting to authority, a feeling they cannot countenance. Therefore, everything they do must be done their way. This attitude sometimes leads to creative acting and indeed may trigger strong motivations. These actors, however, cannot take direction and may willfully destroy their own chances of success in a role. Their problem is that they cannot make good use of ideas offered by the director; naturally, their characterization suffers.

An actor may have such a need to succeed that he cannot acknowledge to himself that his creation is inadequate. The actor feels that it must be good, and consequently he must succeed. It manifests itself in an actor's failure to give up bad acting habits and move on to working methods that are more productive. Somehow, the actor must trust himself so that he can be flexible and capable of making changes. Your task of learning how to become a creative actor is three-fold:

1. You must develop ways of generating information for yourself about all human behavior. You must develop methods of evaluating the materials of human behavior and select those that apply to the character you are portraying.
2. You must learn the methods for using unconscious processes in the service of creating illuminating characters. The methods include the use of incidental learning, confidence in free association, and developing sensitivity to feelings of being "right" or "wrong."
3. You must reach the point where you can remove emotional blocks so that you can achieve any part of the first two learning goals.

To grow as an actor, you must use unconscious procedures for the *acquisition* of elements for future associations. You must develop an acutely sensitive observation apparatus. It is not enough to see the world around you; you must develop an understanding of the "why" of human behavior. Through books, lectures, and experiences through which you acquire relevant information, you consciously increase your fund of information of nature and its nuances and their subtleties. The knowledgeable baseball fan sees an entirely different game from the new spectator—the latter missing the coach's signals, the manager's strategy, the pathos of the has-been; the insightful sensitive observer understands people's hidden motives, catches the subtlety of humor; the mechanic hears the beauty of the motor; the musician hears and feels the symphony—all sense more than laymen who lack a knowledgeable background. Since an actor must create characters from varied cultures, economic strata, and environmental backgrounds, it is essential that you read widely in all the areas of the social sciences, sociology, and psychology. Building a comprehensive background in all aspects of human behavior will make it possible for you to have more relevant elements to utilize in creating a role.

Important as the use of conscious, rational processes is, it does not seem nearly adequate to deal with the actor's need to develop creative ability. Overwhelming evidence indicates that such creation occurs as an unconscious process.

There are methods of getting at knowledge that people are not aware they possess. The psychological literature speaks of incidental learning and latent learning, terms that indicate knowledge acquired without awareness. We get an example of this in those tests given in school that require either a "True" or "False" answer; it is certain that the student is more than 50 percent likely to be right. This likelihood is not accidental, but based on the student's subliminal information, not quite conscious, but expressing itself nonetheless. If the information were conscious, the student would verbalize it and the reason for his selection of that answer. But if he can become sensitized to his bodily feelings, he can also make use of the knowledge that is not yet at the point of verbalization.

The quality of becoming sensitized to bodily states and acquiring confidence in them can be developed. You must become accustomed to your own internal signals. Everything we experience comes to us through our ability to receive messages through our senses. Since you, like almost all actors, wish to please and be pleased, you must be aware that this can influence the nature of the messages you receive through your senses. You need to be keenly aware of how you, yourself, sift sensory evidence.

We are all self-selective in what we meaningfully receive from our senses. Your awareness of this can aid you in being more flexible in your development as an actor.

In addition, you should learn to use free association. This is the technique which involves letting thoughts race through your head uncensored and undirected with the confidence that these thoughts are relevant to your acting needs. Free association can often be used to capture the exact objective of a character at a given moment in a scene if, at the same time, you learn to be aware of your mode of remembering so that you may use it consciously.

The most significant point is that methods exist whereby you may train yourself to become aware of the information you have within yourself, and you may also acquire confidence that your "intuitions" about what you know and feel are usually correct.

The unconscious selectivity practiced by the actor lies again in the internal bodily state. This can be described as an aesthetic sense which is pleased or displeased by a given experience. Some things feel right or wrong without the reasons being apparent. You must develop an awareness that a person has a bodily state and a knowledge of the form that it takes and develop confidence that the bodily state is probably based on information or experience which, when verbalized, would lead to the same conclusion now being signaled by the bodily state.

Creative acts can often be expressed symbolically. Acting may employ symbolic communications such as gestures, sound values including sighing, various kinds of laughter, gasps. All these sounds may communicate more clearly than words. Join your colleagues in a number of exercises that will expand your ability to express symbolically. For example, you may take the figures in a painting, a cartoon, or a newspaper photo and employ them to create a character in a whole dramatic situation. You might decide that such a figure could represent a sexually-thwarted maiden aunt, a self-indulgent rich uncle, a weak father, a positive leader of the people, an earth-mother type.

Perhaps the basic problem you confront in your acting is developing the freedom to release creative potential. This can be done by diminishing the psychological blocks that prevent you from using your emotional and sensory resources. It takes energy to hide, deny, or be blind to one's emotional makeup and needs. This energy may be more productively employed once you accept the nature of yourself and utilize it honestly. The director/teacher may be accused of dealing with the actor's personal life, but it is virtually impossible to separate the actor's psyche from his ability to function as an artist.

As with almost everyone, actors shy away from the term "therapy" which conjures up images of mental illness and weakness. Nonetheless, many of the techniques developed in the therapeutic context, such as free associations and self-insight, have profound implications for the successful actor. The methods that lead to becoming a fine actor and the methods employed in therapy are quite similar; both strive to create conditions under which people change in the direction of growth. It is apparent that methods for removing emotional blocks are related to therapeutic procedures.

While the director/teacher must not play amateur psychologist, nor wish to probe deeply into the actor's psychological makeup, there are various ways of helping the actor in relation to these emotional blocks. The actor and director must recognize that the problems of emotional blocks may be divided into three types:

1. Overcoming the fear of exploring and using the unconscious.
2. Learning how the unconscious works.
3. Feeling free to use it.

As is true of people in all walks of life, some actors fear any venture into the unconscious. They feel that not only will magic powers be found there, but also hostility, lust, and unacceptable behavior from the past. They are certain that opening up the unconscious will make them vulnerable and subject to attack. Further, the prospect of having to confront the unknown is so frightening that they will not permit themselves the freedom to explore the unconscious. Such actors prefer failure to the kind of insight that may lead to success.

Often an inhibition not consciously known to the actor prevents exploration of potential abilities. This inhibition may be attributed to various causes. Perhaps the actor has had a parent who discouraged activity beyond the confines of the usual and socially acceptable. It may be that bursts of affection have been looked upon as frivolous and unbecoming by some authority figure with the concomitant result that the actor fears displays of affection even when they are appropriate to the moment. It is an unfortunate comment on our modes of living that many actors find it easier to express hostility and violence in their work than to express love and warm feelings.

You may find the means of releasing inhibitions of this type by various techniques:

1. Attempting to handle an emotional situation in a manner contrary to your usual procedure.
2. Becoming aware of how other people feel about the same issues and in the same situations.
3. Discovering how people react to the very behavior heretofore you have feared expressing.
4. Permitting yourself to respond to each moment in time in an improvisation without any editing or censoring, regardless of what may emerge. Spontaneous responses are inevitably richer and fuller than intellectual responses. You must guard against blocking natural responses because of fear of a lack of a suitable self-image.

Once the unconscious is available, the problem of expression remains. The social and parental pressures that prevented the expression of needs or abilities at an earlier age also operate in the present. Those who have been discouraged from expressing and acting out their true feelings at an early age will find it difficult to do so later. Childhood disapproval or discouragement will blight or distort an actor's creativity. For the actor to achieve flexibility and freedom, these original inhibiting forces must be removed. It is a source of constant wonderment to actors that, when they release these inhibiting forces, they are almost always praised by their colleagues for their improved performance; the positive benefits and reaction of other actors to creative work and the realization of their human potential will accelerate the growth of the actor.

CHAPTER 2

DEVELOPING RELAXATION AND FREEDOM

One of the first things you must achieve to become a fine actor is a relaxed body that is pliant and responsive to the physical qualities and emotions of the character you are playing. Secondly, you must place yourself in a physical and mental state that makes it possible for you to use your sensory-emotional resources without censorship or editing. Sensory resources are simply those elements Stanislavsky discussed in "Sense Memory" that include touching, seeing, hearing, tasting, and smelling. Emotional resources are all those elements of feeling that have been experienced and remembered in what Stanislavsky called "Affective Memory" and Richard Boleslavsky described more accurately as "Memory of Emotion." The use of the word "memory" is somewhat misleading since it allows the actor the safety of distance in "remembering." Perhaps a better word to use would be "re-experiencing" so that the use of the sensory-emotional resources would again become a here-and-now happening.

For these reasons, included here are a number of possible freedom-relaxation exercises that are most helpful to the actor. These should be experienced in the first acting sessions and then may be repeated briefly at subsequent sessions. The entire acting group should participate simultaneously in the exercises so that no part of the group is observing other students acting during the exercise. Observation of these exercises by outsiders should be discouraged. With all the actors working concurrently, self-consciousness is minimized and the individual actor's possibility of success is enhanced.

Your first sessions should be concerned exclusively with sensory recall and physical responses to stimuli. After some success has been achieved in these areas, the exercise can then be expanded to involve your use of past emotional experiences. These freedom-relaxation exercises should become more complicated as you increasingly trust your sense memory and allow yourself to re-experience emotional episodes from your life.

In these exercises the teacher-director may frequently employ *side-coaching.* This is a process that can be described as a series of verbal suggestions given while the exercise is in progress. In the event you are side-coached by the teacher-director, do not break concentration or interrupt the progress of the action in which you are engaged. You should incorporate the suggestions given without stopping or interrupting the action.

At the commencement of these exercises, there are three stages through which you move to obtain relaxation. They are:

1. Standing with your feet approximately six inches apart, you lean back stretching your back, arm, and leg muscles tightly.
2. On the teacher-director command, "Collapse," you drop forward from the waist so that your head and torso face the floor. You should feel as though your body is hanging by a string attached to the lower part of your vertebrae. Your back should be so relaxed that the teacher-director can sway your body in any direction. If there is any muscular tension or physical rigidity in any part of your body, you should begin the exercise again. Muscular tension is evidence that you are trying to control your situation, and this mitigates the value of the exercise.
3. On the command, "Inhale," breathing through an open mouth you slowly inflate your lungs with air, concurrently bringing your body up piece by piece along the vertebrae until you reach an erect position. Your body should reach its erect position at the same moment that your lungs are filled to their maximum capacity. At this point you let the air out through your open mouth and begin breathing normally. From this point onward you should attempt to maintain a neutral mental state as well as a completely relaxed body until you are side-coached. Mental neutrality can be defined as allowing yourself a mental status in

which you neither think about, manipulate, or attempt to control your existing situation. If you are aware that you are trying to control your physical and mental choices, begin the exercise again.

Once you are relaxed physically, have achieved a neutral mental status, and are responsive intuitively to the side-coaching, you are ready to begin the second phase of the exercise. You are now ready to deal with the relatively simple problem in which your sense memory plays the most significant part. Sense memory is the re-experiencing of your reaction to such sensual stimuli as touching, smelling, tasting, seeing, and hearing. During this portion of the exercise you should avoid "indicating"—the practice of externalizing your feeling before you have actually re-experienced from out of your past some appropriate specific feeling. You must not concern yourself with "showing" us what your feeling is. Instead, your re-experiencing is to be as complete as possible; out of the ensuing recall will come actions, activities, and responses that will naturally reveal the feelings you experienced.

Here is an example of how such an exercise might work. The teacher-director side-coaches, "You are as hot as you've ever been in your life."

You and the other actors in the exercise, each employing their own sense memory, begin re-experiencing an episode in their individual lives when they were very hot and trying to keep as cool as possible. After it is obvious that each of the actors is physically suffering from the heat, the teacher-director may signal out individual actors and question them. One such conversation might be:

Teacher-Director

Where are you?

Actor

On a fishing boat.

Teacher-Director

Who is with you?

Actor

I'm alone.

Teacher-Director

Why are you here?

Actor

I can't get the boat started
. . . it's stalled and there is
no one around to help.

Teacher-Director

What time is it?

Actor

(not sure)
About two . . . I think.

The teacher-director then might move on to another student who is participating in the exercise and ask him/her similar questions with different responses based on his/her sense memory.

As these freedom-relaxation exercises progress, it will be natural for you to not only have sense memories but also to experience memory of emotion. An example of such experiencing in which the emotional recall is paramount is given in the following dialogue between an actor and the teacher-director:

Teacher-Director

Where are you?

Actor

I'm in my bedroom.

Teacher-Director

Are you alone?

Actor

Yes.

Teacher-Director

What time is it?

Actor

A little after midnight. . . .
No! More like two in the morning.

Teacher-Director

Does anyone know you're crying?

Actor

My mother and father.

Teacher-Director

Do they care?

Actor

No!
(after a moment)
No . . . that's not true! I'm
not sure . . . I think they
think I'm being childish.

During the exercise the teacher-director may ask you whatever questions will trigger your complete re-experiencing of an incident from the past. For the memory of emotion to be successful, you must reply as honestly as possible to these questions in the context of your recalled environment and situation.

It is important for you to answer all questions in the present tense. In utilizing sensory and emotional recall it is imperative that you re-experience the incident and not filter it through your mind with accompanying censoring as a remembered incident. There is a vast difference between re-experiencing and remembering. When side-coaching or asking you questions, the teacher-director must always speak in the present tense. It is interesting to observe those actors who consistently choose to reply in the past tense. They are attempting to establish an emotional distance between themselves and the experience; they are actually attempting to avoid the present tense "I am" by substituting the safer "I was" or "I did." This tendency to translate emotional recall into the past tense is done so that the actor can keep a little part of himself outside the situation; such actors may feel that they must behave well according to their idea of what constitutes proper social behavior. They are constantly manipulating their emotional reactions to conform to what they believe is a desired code of behavior.

Freedom-relaxation exercises may have endless variations. These are a few examples:

1. The teacher-director side-coaches, "On command, you will collapse to the floor falling into a deep, dark, abandoned mine shaft." After a moment the teacher-director shouts, "Fall!" The actors plummet to the floor as they fall into the imagined mine shaft. After a few moments some may start to solve the problem of being trapped in a mine shaft. Others may choose to be hurt and not able to do much more than deal with the resulting pain. Perhaps another actor may suffer from claustrophobia. One by one, all the actors must deal with the problem of being trapped in a mine shaft and look for solutions to their dilemma. Primarily the recall element of the exercise is of a physical nature; emotional recall may become part of the exercise as it evolves out of the sensory recall. Since it is unlikely that you or any of the other actors have actually experienced falling into a mine shaft, you need to make what is called a "transference." For example, you might re-experience a time when you were injured. You may re-experience a time when you were confined in a dark, claustrophobic place. What child has not experienced the fear of the dark before falling asleep? You can certainly transfer such experiences into the dilemma of being in an abandoned mine shaft. You may re-experience the fear that accompanies being caught in a physical dilemma that may not have ready solutions. All of these recalled experiences are applicable to what you probably would feel if you fell into an abandoned mine shaft.

2. The teacher-director side-coaches, "You are to re-experience a time in your life when you are very hot and suffering much discomfort." Once the actors have established a very real experiencing of the heat, the exercise may progress another step. The teacher-director may then suggest to the actors that they group together in close proximity, keeping their feelings of experienc-

ing intense heat and discomfort. When they are huddled together the teacher-director may side-coach, "You are on a life raft in a listless sea with almost all your water supply gone." After awhile the teacher-director may add, "You hear a rescue plane. It is coming close." You and the other actors will naturally respond to all of this side-coaching. Perhaps a few moments later the teacher-director says, "The rescue plane doesn't see you. It is flying away."

In evaluating your success or failure in the exercise, ask yourself if you remained true to the environment and sensory circumstances once emotional elements entered into the exercise. Has the low water supply resulted in your throat being parched and your voice hoarse? Have you been physically exhausted? From this exercise you and your fellow actors may have evolved distinct characterizations and varying reactions to the problems.

3. The teacher-director side-coaches, "You are to recall a time in your life when you are as cold as you have ever been."

4. The teacher-director side-coaches, "It is wartime; for some reason you are in the middle of a combat zone during the hostile action."

5. The teacher-director side-coaches, "Your dearest friend is swimming in the ocean. You don't know how to swim." After a moment during which the actors have established that they are very much part of the environment at the beach and are enjoying their surroundings, the teacher-director may continue to side-coach, "Suddenly your friend develops a cramp and calls for your help. You throw your friend a lifeline. You are trying to pull your friend ashore although the tide is heavy and difficult." The teacher-director spaces out this side-coaching so that the actors can incorporate each new idea into their situation. As the actors concern themselves with these activities the teacher-director may then side-coach, "Put more muscle into it! . . . You're not feeling the weight!" After a moment the teacher-director might shout, "You lose hold of the rope!" In this case the rope may or may not be permanently lost by the actors; you decide for

yourself whether you catch the rope at the last moment or lose it. Your friend may be swept out to sea and drown. You may or may not save your friend. In these exercises you make your own choices, and your spontaneous responses to the varied side-coaching is most helpful in teaching you to trust your intuitions.

6. The teacher-director side-coaches, "You are to carry a valuable object from one location to another." Perhaps in the midst of this exercise the teacher-director side-coaches, "Stumble!"

7. The teacher-director side-coaches, "You are involved in a very dirty, physically demanding job in which the accompanying noise is loud and relentless."

Significantly, whatever you emotionally experience will evolve out of the sensory situation; you must first of all deal with the activities, objectives, and environment central to the situation. You need not concern yourself with emotions or the need to reveal an emotional state. Whatever emotions evolve are a natural result of your character's experience while seeking your objective, dealing with those activities appropriate to the situation and working within the specific environment.

Once you have begun to successfully use your sensory resources within the freedom-relaxation exercises, it is time to make use of your emotional resources. By this time you have probably begun to trust your intuitions and are prepared to let whatever you are experiencing evolve without self-censoring. Under no circumstances should the teacher-director permit you and the other actors to sidestep such emotional experiencing. It is essential that you permit yourself to be vulnerable if you are to become a fine actor. The third phase of the freedom-relaxation exercise may include many emotional experiences. For example, the teacher-director may side-coach, "You are to re-experience a time in your life when you are as angry as you have ever been!" Once your re-experiencing is developing satisfactorily, the teacher-director may then side-coach, "Pick up an imaginary rock and throw it!" If you simply go through the motions without your anger being real and thus convincing, the teacher-director may continue side-coaching, "HARDER!" "BREAK IT!" "STAMP ON IT!" "SAY WHAT YOU WANT!" The teacher-director should keep after the actors until their anger is real and truly experienced.

Some actors will claim that they have never experienced anger. Possibly saints have not experienced anger, but it is certainly not true of ordinary human beings. Anger is a natural part of the human condition. If you or other actors have trouble experiencing anger, the teacher-director must delve into aspects of the actor's experiencing until the teacher-director finds that moment when anger was truly felt even though its overt expression may have been repressed at the time. The actor must be forced to give vent to his/her anger in a physical and overt manner regardless of how he or she expressed or repressed anger at the time.

The teacher-director may side-coach, "You are to recall a time in your life when you realize you are falling in love." For many actors this exercise will be a joyful re-experiencing. For others the teacher-director may need to side-coach, "The excitement, the pleasure, the joy of not being alone, but part of someone else's life should sweep over you." A few moments later the teacher-director may side-coach, "Touch the person you love." For some actors falling in love may remain something not yet experienced. In this case they should employ the "Magic If." By this phrase we mean "Imagine yourself in the situation." Although you may not yet have experienced love, it is highly probable that you have fantasized the possibility of falling in love and you can use this imagined experience.

The teacher-director supervising the freedom-relaxation exercises should allow the actors all the time that is necessary for them to re-experience a specific incident. Once it appears that the actors are recalling a specific moment in time, the teacher-director may then ask the actors individually such questions as "Where are you?" "What time is it?" "Are you alone?" "Who is with you?" "Did you expect this to happen?"

The teacher-director may side-coach, "You are to re-experience a time in your life when you are responsible for hurting someone you love very much." After the memory of emotion is being experienced, the teacher-director may ask, "Is there any thing you can do to change your situation?" The actor may respond to this question as though this thought was running through their stream of consciousness. The teacher-director might follow this response with, "Is this your fault?" "Where is the person now?" "Are you going to say something to the person you love?" If the reply to this question is "Yes," the teacher-director may side-coach, "All right! Do it!" The actor may then re-experience as completely as possible whatever it is that he or she said and did.

The teacher-director may side-coach, "You are to recall a time when you were a child celebrating with great pleasure some specific occasion." After the memory of emotion is being re-experienced, the teacher-director may ask questions which will help the actor's experience to be recalled as completely as possible. For example, this dialogue between the actor and the teacher-director might occur:

Teacher-Director

What'cha doing, Bill?

Actor

Hiding.

Teacher-Director

Who you hiding from?

Actor

Dad.

Teacher-Director

Does he know where you are?

Bill shakes his head, "No."

Teacher-Director

Is he looking around for you?

Bill nods his head affirmatively.

Teacher-Director

Do you think he'll find you?

Once again Bill nods, "No."

Successful in his memory of emotion, Bill's responses have become those of a child delighting in secrecy; he whispers all his answers and sometimes uses only actions to respond. Another actress, questioned, might respond in this way:

Teacher-Director

Where are you, Sharon?

Actor

I'm playing marbles.

Teacher-Director

You're playing marbles! Girls
aren't supposed to play marbles!

Actor

They let me.

Teacher-Director

Who?

Actor

The kids let me.

Teacher-Director

They think you're any good?

Actor

Yeah . . . I beat them . . .

Teacher-Director

You beat them!?

Actor

Sure!

Teacher-Director

Did you win any?

The actor extends her hand holding imaginary marbles.

Actor

I got ten!

Teacher-Director

Ten!

Actor

Yeah! Real big ones!

At no time during the freedom-relaxation exercises should the teacher-director offer criticism. The teacher-director's value lies wholly within the emotional-sensory situations that he/she sets up for the actors to re-experience. The way in which the teacher-director participates both as a questioner and sometimes as a character can also be of enormous value to the ultimate success of these exercises. During the exercises the teacher-director may side-coach:

PHYSICALIZE!

DON'T JUST TALK ABOUT IT!

LET'S SEE IT!

LET'S HEAR YOUR SIDE OF THE CONVERSATION . . . TALK TO THE PERSON JUST AS YOU DID!

KEEP YOUR ENVIRONMENT WORKING!

YOU'RE INDICATING!

At the conclusion of the exercise the actors will be aware of the degree of their individual success. You will know how well you have done so that the teacher-director's comments are superfluous and should be minimized. The actors' success will result from continued application of the exercises rather than from critical commentary.

Some other emotional-sensory recall situations that may be employed in the freedom-relaxation exercises are:

1. "You dread doing something you don't want to do."
2. "You are receiving praise for something you have done well."
3. "You are being belittled, and your value as a person is being ridiculed."

4. "You are concerned that you have hurt someone you love."
5. "You are faced with an unfamiliar environment in which you are not comfortable."
6. "You are re-experiencing an emotion that you consider despicable in yourself."
7. "You are re-experiencing a time when you feel raunchy, unworthy, uncouth, and immoral."

These are recall situations that you probably can draw upon from specific moments in your life. The following possible situations would call upon you to use the "Magic If."

1. "You are a visitor to the state penitentiary. You are there to witness the death of a prisoner in the gas chamber. You are sitting in the press box along with other observers. You have come to know the prisoner who is to be executed; you know the prisoner to be guilty. However, under other circumstances, you believe that the prisoner could have been a wonderful human being. You value the prisoner and now consider him/her a friend. After a few moments the teacher-director might add, "The prisoner sees you . . . he/she is trying to tell you something . . . You can't hear the prisoner through the glass partition . . . You want the prisoner to know that you care for him/her. After a few moments the teacher-director might side-coach, "The gas chamber pellets fall." A few moments later, "The prisoner is dead."
2. "You are in a snow-bound cabin high in the mountains. A violent storm is raging outside, and even indoors it is cold. The building creaks under the weight of the storm. Inside the cabin you are watching a woman in labor; she will soon give birth to a child."
3. "You are leafing through an old cardboard box filled with momentos. You find something that makes you remember someone out of your past, someone very meaningful to you but half-forgotten in your daily activities."
4. "You are caught in an earthquake. . . . You see a wall of bricks falling down on someone you love."
5. "You are caught on the deck of a ship during the middle of a typhoon . . . You see someone important to you swept overboard."

Once you have begun working in these exercises successfully, you will discover that you are usually no longer concerned with such problems as "What shall I do with my hands?" or "How do I walk from here to there?" The anxiety of using your body effectively will have been largely eliminated. Once you clearly understand what you are experiencing at a given moment and focus on it with total absorption, the body responds automatically and usually correctly to whatever stimuli it encounters. You will have also discovered that, when you trust your intuitions and allow your emotions to be expressed without censoring or editing, those emotions will seem valid and true to the observer. You will have begun to achieve the relaxation and freedom in your work so essential to becoming an effective actor.

CHAPTER 3

THE TOOLS OF ACTING

Just as a carpenter uses hammer, saw, and plane, an actor has tools at his disposal that can make his work much more successful. Before you undertake acting in structured scenes, you need to identify these tools and learn how to use them through the exercises described in this chapter. These acting tools are concentration, observation, memory of emotion, rhythm, characterization, and sense memory.

CONCENTRATION

For you as an actor, concentration means that your attention is focused entirely on obtaining what your character wants. You believe totally in your environment and the circumstances in which your character is placed. Your attention is not on the audience, but on focusing all energy toward obtaining your character's objectives. Concentration implies total absorption in obtaining what your character wants, only giving up that objective when it is no longer prudent, or when you have learned new information that changes your character's goal. In the course of pursuing your character's objectives, you may be forced to overcome obstacles, find the justification for your character's goals, and make adaptations as a result of new information, or the changing of relationships. Your performance will not be self-conscious, but believable if you surrender your personal being to the character you are playing. It is total attention to what your character wants and the pursuance of those wants that will make your characterization believable and natural.

OBSERVATION

You must notice everything unusual and out of the ordinary in everyday life. You should put into your memory bank all the actions, feelings, and responses to humankind that you have seen so that when any of them are applicable to a role you are playing you have these resources upon which to draw.

The person you are playing may come from a very different social and cultural background than your own. Observe the movement of many different people; there is much to be gained by merely looking and noting the way people use their bodies. Watch how they look, touch, and react to being touched. While emulating people you have observed in life situations that may not be "natural" to you, it will automatically make the character you create more natural to the audience. If you use Stanislavsky's tool of observation, you will soon discover that people vary greatly in the way they use their bodies to communicate. Some have a wide, expansive range of movement accompanied by similar gestures and facial expressions. Others may have a very narrow range of movement; they may have small, tight movements and try to keep their face a mask free of emotion. All this observation should result in assisting you to find the appropriate movement for the character you are playing. The movement of the people you observe is motivated by their individual psyche, and you must probe this psyche to understand the quality of their movement. Finally, you must ask yourself, "Why does this person move this way? What is her psychological makeup that makes her automatically expansive or small and tight?" The body has a language of its own that often is most helpful in telling you something about a character.

You should also observe the many ways that people reveal aspects of their psychological makeup by their voices. Are they quick or slow to respond? Are they hasty or measured in their judgments? Do they reveal confidence or uncertainty in their questions and statements? Do they employ a great many sounds other than words that help convey their emotional feelings? The sighs, groans, laughter, snorts, fast inhaling of air and slow exhaling may all tell us as much about a character as any words that person may speak.

Observation will open your eyes to the similarities and the differences in human behavior from one individual to another. You should not only assess the "what" of human actions, but also the "why" of these actions.

MEMORY OF EMOTION

One of the ways in which you can find the appropriate emotions for a scene is to awaken in your memory an episode in your life where your emotional experiencing has a correlation to the emotions required for the scene. Recalling that emotion, you can "transfer" it to your character's experiencing in the scene. Sometimes the best way to achieve this "affective memory" is to concentrate on the physical details and incidental circumstances which surrounded the emotional moment; recalling your physical surroundings; remembering the incidental sounds that existed at the time of the experiencing; seeing in your mind's eye the people who were there during the event, are all useful in the emotional incident being re-experienced. As you begin to learn how to use your memory of emotion, you will discover that emotion is the result of things that you have thought and experienced and not the result of trying to show emotion. When recapturing past emotional experiences, it is important that you be aware of what the stimulus was at that time and how that stimulus triggered what you wanted to do and what you felt.

Whenever an actor works with such generalized clichés as "love," "hate," or "anger," he is doomed to failure. If you have understood your character, concerned yourself with the inner action of your character, pursued your character's objective legitimately and honestly, and applied appropriate experiences from out of your own life that relate to the character you are playing, it is inevitable that your feelings will be genuine and believable to the audience.

Sometimes you will be able to quickly identify with the character you are playing and find that you have a storehouse of feelings immediately available to you. Sometimes it will be necessary to probe into your past and re-experience an incident that can be applied to what your character is experiencing. Regardless, you should always be concerned with *playing your action* so that whatever feeling takes place within the scene varies according to what you are experiencing at that moment in time. The noted director Harold Clurman pointed out that "you must deal with each moment in time for its own value" and that the sum total of those moments would be both your character and what your character is feeling.

You must guard against hanging onto an emotion beyond the moment when it is truly experienced by you. If you hang onto such an emotion it is because you are not really listening, interacting, or seeing clearly the changing life around you.

Looking for an emotional reference in your own life that is appropriate for your character is sometimes called "personalization." When you have discovered an occasion from your own life that in some ways parallels what your character is experiencing, you then proceed to relive it in your imagination. You look for the stimuli that caused your emotional experiencing. When, where, why, how did it occur? Examine exactly what took place step by step and then incorporate what is appropriate into your character. This "personalization," incorporating your character's emotional experiencing into your own past experience, can lead to a rich and wholly believable characterization.

RHYTHM

Perceiving the use of rhythm as an actor is to understand that it consists in developing a sensitivity to rhythm and not to learning to move rhythmically. Rhythm should be perceived as coming from within. It is the actor finding in his character the appropriate rhythm in the movement of his body, of his mind, and of his feelings. If you perceive the rhythm of a character, it means that you understand the role. The same actor will find very different rhythms central to his character if he is playing such diverse roles as "Hamlet," "Tartuffe," or "Willy Loman." Further, the actor must be aware that not only does his character have a special kind of rhythm but so does the drama itself; to find the rhythm of a drama is to find the key to its presentation.

CHARACTERIZATION

An actor is inevitably boring and predictable if he does not have the imagination to see that each character he creates from a script is unique and different from any other character. There is a great difference between finding within yourself the appropriate emotional, sensory, and physical resources applicable to your character and altering the part to fit your most comfortable resources. In creating a role you should always ask yourself, "What is the difference between myself and the character as it is described by the playwright?" You will learn about some of those characteristics of the person you are playing from many sources: what the dramatist states specifically about your character, what other characters say about your character, how other characters seem to respond to your character. It is the actor's task to discover the main psychological characteristics of the person he is playing and then find the means of illuminating them to the audience.

In creating any character, your whole being must be changed psychologically and physically. This change is not grotesque; it may only be of a small degree, but it is a change from your own being. Once you have found the psychological truth within your character, you then look for those manners of speech, movement, and habit that set your character apart in his uniqueness. The whole character seems to come alive, more human and true as soon as you have found the vocal and physical qualities that illuminate his psychological makeup.

In the early stages of creating the character, you must not be afraid of failure. You must explore many possibilities within the character. Some of this probing may lead you to make choices that eventually you will discard. You must not be afraid of taking risks that may seem foolish or even misguided; these risks may lead you to insights valuable to the character. Part of your characterization may reveal aspects of your own inner life; you must not be afraid that these revelations will make you vulnerable.

It is also important not to feel the need to freeze your character too early in the course of the rehearsals. Stay flexible. Allow your character to change as you make new discoveries during the "give and take" between your character and the other characters in the play. While you must begin rehearsals with a clear-cut notion of what your character's objectives are, it is also important that you be sensitive to the moment-to-moment stimuli around you. Your character's intentions will remain a constant, but the many shadings and nuances that evolve in your characterization are a result of your reaction to the way other characters in the script choose to behave and respond to your character. As the characters evolve during the rehearsal period, many influences will help to alter and shape your characterization: the way another character listens or fails to listen to you; the intonation of her voice which may convey something quite different from the words she is speaking; the way her body communicates sympathetically or negatively to you. All of these different actions, many of which you cannot have anticipated in the initial reading of the script, will and should change your concept of the character from the notions that you started with at the beginning of rehearsal.

In the early stages of rehearsal do not feel the need to discuss your character with the other actors. In all probability the director will have begun rehearsals with a discussion of the spine of the script, the character's objectives, and all those aspects of production pertinent to the actor's understanding. From then on during the early stages of rehearsal I do not feel it's a good idea to discuss your character with other actors. After all, in life situations it is rare that we explain ourselves to others or give reasons for the actions we take. I have found that imaginative creative work is not helped, but hindered, by discussion. There are actors who "talk a good part" so that unconsciously they do not have to "play a good part." Later in rehearsals, once the actors have already created the experience and are now communicating it, discussions between the actors can result in deeper shadings and nuances that can be helpful.

SENSE MEMORY

Sense memory is the actor's use of any or all of his five senses as appropriate to the character in his environment. Re-experiencing what you have seen, heard, smelled, tasted, or touched can be most helpful in validating a character you are playing. For example, the chill and exhaustion an actor might recall having experienced during and after a hunting trip may be an appropriate "sense recall" if the actor is called upon to play a political prisoner enclosed in a barren cell.

In creating a character in a script, you can use sensory details to give new life to a remembered experience; they can trigger not only the feeling of the original event but help you to use physical actions appropriate to whatever your character should be doing. You should rely, whenever possible, on your own experiences, recalling details that will cause you to produce actions that you might not otherwise consider. In recapturing a sensory experience that you feel somewhat parallels the experiences of the character you are playing, you should ask yourself these questions: (1) When did it happen? 2) Why did it happen? (3) What were the conditions under which it happened? (4) Where did it happen and what was the nature of the surroundings in which it happened? (5) What did I do when it happened?

Choosing sensory recall that gives your character believability within your environment is an important and frequently overlooked task necessary if you wish to be an effective actor.

The following exercises are designed to assist you in developing the tools of Concentration, Observation, Memory of Emotion, Rhythm, Characterization, and Sense Memory.

INANIMATE OBJECTS

This exercise in portraying inanimate objects will assist you in developing the tools of concentration, observation, and use of rhythm.

This is a simple basic exercise in which you work singly. You are to capture as completely as possible the qualities of some kind of inanimate object that is acted upon by outside forces. For example, you might portray an elevator that is being used by people. In portraying the characteristics of an elevator, you should not attempt to take on human qualities; we are not interested in seeing the elevator with a "human personality." Instead, you should concern yourself exclusively with capturing the physical attributes of the elevator. Those observing you should be able to recognize the inanimate object that you are portraying. For example, those watching you should be able to tell from your depiction whether you are an automatic elevator that is self-operating or whether you are maneuvered from floor to floor by a person. Strictly through your movement you should be able to convey to the observer what inanimate object you are portraying. In the past we have observed actors portray such diverse inanimate objects as ice cubes in a highball glass, a tumbleweed out on the plains, an egg frying, the ocean, plants growing, a windmill, an electric sign in Times Square, bubble gum.

IMAGINATION

This exercise in imagination will assist you in developing the tools of concentration, sense memory, memory of emotion, and characterization.

This imagination exercise employs some of the same characteristics that actors encounter in improvisations. The dialogue comes out of the free associations of the actors; it is not pre-planned. However, these exercises are designed for a different purpose. They are intended to stretch your creative imagination and assist you in discovering the means of illuminating a dramatic situation, your innermost feelings, including your sub-text at the time of the action, and your relationship to your environment. Consequently, the actors have at their disposal considerable information that is denied to them when they are working in improvisations.

Prior to the exercise, working with another actor, you should exchange information and structure the dramatic event so that it has a beginning, a middle, and an end. Further, you may do considerable pre-planning as to the actions and activities that will transpire during the exercise. You and your acting partner should make several choices which are to prevail during the exercise:

1. You must establish an environment that is unique and make this atmosphere known to the audience without either of you alluding to it specifically in the dialogue. For example, a unique environment might be a cold storage room of a meat packing plant, or an abandoned warehouse in the middle of the night.
2. The characters you and your acting partner are playing may or may not know each other at the beginning of the exercise, but a meaningful relationship must be established between you during the course of the action.
3. During the exercise an important action must take place that will alter the circumstances of your life and your relationship to each other.

Here is an example: It is late at night as a man fumbles for keys and puts them into a lock. Turning the key, he opens the door and enters a dark house. Inside he stumbles on some furniture, is surprised, and then realizes that the room has been rearranged since he was last here. Cautiously he moves through the house. He stops at a door, quietly enters, views a small child asleep. The actor makes us know that he sees a small child by his actions including re-covering the child with a blanket that has slipped during the night. Then, after a moment, he leaves the bedroom and moves to another area that we soon can tell from his actions is the kitchen. Searching through a drawer, he finds a butcher knife, pulls it out, and heads to another room. As he gets to the door he is confronted by a woman holding a gun. He realizes that he is trapped; she realizes that he has come with the intent of killing her. As they both stare at each other with mixtures of surprise and fear, he suddenly turns the knife on himself and falls to the floor—dead.

This particular imagination exercise was done without any dialogue. However, if it is appropriate, the actors should feel free to use dialogue.

DECISION

This decision exercise will assist you in developing the tools of concentration, sense memory, and, most importantly, memory of emotion.

This exercise has some of the elements of improvisation inasmuch as it does not have structured dialogue or a planned beginning, middle, or end. Furthermore, the acting participants have no pre-conceived notion of the exercise's outcome.

First, choose another actor in the acting workshop to play a character whose goodwill and approval are most important to the character you are playing. This significant person could be someone such as your spouse, lover, father, mother, employer, or best friend. In any event, it must be a person whose relationship to you and feelings about you are of great concern to you. Just before the improvisational-type exercise begins, you inform your acting partner of his relationship to you, reveal any circumstances of the past that are necessary to his understanding of what is taking place, and the locale and time of the event about to transpire. Under no circumstances do you reveal to him any elements of the decision you are making; that decision must be revealed during the action of the exercise.

Once the decision exercise begins, you must reveal to your acting partner the decision that you have made and then, in subsequent action, attempt to convince, justify, or make understood why you have made such a decision. While you recognize that your decision will inevitably alter your relationship to the other person, you cannot anticipate how that person will react to your decision. Her reaction to you may have myriad possibilities: anger and estrangement, love and support, hurt, elation, incredulity, shock, despair, guilt at some sin they imagine that they have brought upon you; the responses are endless in their variety.

Here are some examples:

1. The decision of a young man to evade the draft in a country where most people sympathize with the war objectives.
2. The decision of a person to step outside the acceptable sexual mores of his society.
3. The decision of a person to leave an organized religious institution in which the person has played an important part. The person is leaving that institution for another and opposing cause.

4. The decision of an individual to take an unpopular and, in the view of many, reprehensible political stand.

IMAGERY CHARACTERIZATION

This exercise will assist you in developing the tools of concentration, observation, rhythm, and sense memory.

Sometimes an actor will feel stymied in his attempts to capture those traits that will enhance and give a character color. When you experience such blocks, one method of discovering traits in a character that you may have overlooked is the employment of imagery. When we hear the descriptive phrase, "he eats like a horse!" we immediately conjure up an image of a certain kind of voracious, probably gross individual. Images can prove a valuable "trigger" to you when you are trying to find a character's behavior patterns. The following exercise is designed so that you will employ an "image" which dominates your personality. Once an "image" has been suggested, you should move around, engage in conversations with others, and involve yourself in activities which reflect the characteristics of your selected image.

Here are some possible images:

champagne bubbling

cigarette smoldering

red silk material rustling in the dark

rubber ball bouncing on the floor

the insistent dripping of water into a half-filled saucepan

a power saw whose momentum is interrupted from time to time

a 78 rpm record, worn out, dusty, but still in use

a 33 1/3 record of a girl singer played at 45 rpm

a religious candle flickering in a red glass

a listless old overhead fan in a tropics bar

dishes clattering on a restaurant floor

termites clicking in a decrepit house

an old wooden stove that has gotten red on the sides from overheating

musty, dusty law books in a turn-of-the century law office

roar of the football crowd at the stadium on an October Saturday

strumming of a guitar by a non-musical singer

glacier ice cap crumbling away and moving relentlessly

It is recommended that you be able to prepare yourself for this exercise at least a day before the assignment is done in the workshop. During this interim period you are encouraged to use the "image" you have selected as an influence on you as you participate in the ordinary events of your life. For example, you may during the course of your day mow the lawn, read a newspaper, take the dog for a walk, wash the dishes, visit with a friend, type a letter. During these events you should allow your sense of the "image" to influence the manner in which you participate in these activities. You must keep in mind what your responses, reactions, movement, and manner of speaking will be when strongly influenced by the "image" you have selected or been given.

When you meet with your fellow actors to work on these image exercises, the director-teacher may choose several improvisatory situations in which the actor will work utilizing the influence of the "image." Here is an example:

The actor given the image is to come into a retail store to purchase an item. The kind of store and the goods it sells may be determined by the actor who will convey this information to his acting partner who will play the sales clerk. He may ask the clerk to give him some item, perhaps look at a number of items for sale, finally choose a particular piece of merchandise. All sorts of variations between a customer and a salesperson may take place. Perhaps the customer may request that the item be gift wrapped. The customer may discover that he has left his money at home. He may completely change his mind as to what merchandise he wishes to buy. In any event, his strong sense of image should dominate the proceedings and be a major influence on his characterization.

SEPARATE ELEMENTS

This exercise will assist you in developing the tools of observation, characterization, sense memory, concentration, and rhythm.

Too often actors have not developed an understanding of the exact tools that combine into the art of acting. Several different elements may enter into a single scene; all of them enhance the audience's grasp of the character and situation. There is considerable difference, for example, between the actor's choice of his character's objective and the simultaneous activities in which the character may be engaged. A demonstration of the separate elements of objectivity and activity can be seen in a couple who may be plotting a murder while concurrently dancing in a pleasant, wholesome atmosphere. Combining such diverse elements certainly adds to the irony and, perhaps, the horror of their intent.

The plotting of the murder is the couple's *objective.*

The carefree dancing is their *activity.*

The pleasant, wholesome atmosphere is their *environment.*

Film director Alfred Hitchcock used this odd juxtaposition of a character's objectives and his concurrent activity with great effect. In NORTH BY NORTHWEST he deliberately chose a bland landscape, a peaceful wheat field, for one of his most suspenseful scenes. His hero is nonchalantly walking along a deserted two-lane highway. Without any forewarning, a crop-dusting plane that has been established in the background suddenly looms towards the hero, its flyer mercilessly bent on mowing down the hero. In this particular instance the actor and director matched objectives and activities in such a manner that the action could still be a valid statement of human behavior. The audience must be able to accept the objective and its concurrent activity as possible behavior.

These are the separate elements that must be combined in this exercise:

1. You must choose your objective.
2. You then choose three different activities that you must do while pursuing your objective.
3. You then establish more than one condition of your environment. For example, it is cold, wet, and incredibly silent.
4. You may, if you wish, add a physical problem. For example, you may be crippled or blind.

Ideally, you should repeat the exercise several times, concentrating each time on one or more of the elements. The first time you may concentrate on only the first two elements: your objective and three activities. On repeating the exercise you may add the third element: three conditions of your environment. A third turn-through of the exercise might combine all four elements.

Here is an example:

An estranged husband sneaks into the darkened home of his wife with the objective of killing her. His activities might include finding a key that will open the door, putting on gloves so that he will not leave fingerprints, searching through the kitchen drawers for a suitable weapon. The conditions of his environment might include moving in total darkness, discovering that the furniture has been rearranged since he lived there, trying to see his small child sleeping in her bedroom. A creative actor might add the physical problem of being under the influence of liquor which has helped to prompt him to his objective.

Here is another example using more than one actor:

A married couple meet some people in a bar and invite them to stop by their home for a nightcap drink. Once in the house, the strangers tie up and blindfold the couple. In the struggle the husband's toe is broken. The strangers then proceed to systematically rob and ransack the house leaving the furniture upturned and the house in chaos. As the action begins, the tied-up, blindfolded couple is struggling to get into a room where there is a telephone so that they can call the police. The teacher-director may have hidden the telephone in the room so that it will be difficult to find. The couple's struggle is great since they are tied back-to-back to each other and they cannot see what they are doing.

GIBBERISH

This exercise will assist you in developing the tools of concentration, rhythm, sense memory, and characterization.

When an audience watches a film in a language unknown to them, it is not difficult to follow the action provided the acting is of sufficient merit. Sub-titles are useful but not necessary for comprehension. Vocal inflection, facial actions, body mannerisms, and physical action in the Western world tend to be universal in meaning. The fine actor employs all these instruments in capturing and illuminating a character to the audience. For these reasons it is interesting to see what happens when an actor is deprived of language as a means of communicating his character's objectives and emotions. That actor who becomes incapable of communicating his objectives and the accompanying emotions relevant to those objectives is making minimal use of his body, face, and the sound values implicit in words that distinguish the accomplished actor.

Gibberish exercises can be very helpful to you in developing your voice, body, and face as instruments of your art. In these exercises you are not permitted to use recognizable words. Instead you use combinations of make-believe words in addition to using your body, your face, and the varied sounds you bring to these gibberish words to convey your objectives and your feelings at the moment. For example, you may use a combination of "Me-mo's, "Ling-Lings," and har-de-da-la-vay-toes" into a semblance of sentences which to the audience may seem as though they were hearing an actor speaking a foreign language. What is important in the exercise is not whether you make ingenious use of a combination of pseudo-words but whether you are capable of communicating, in a believable way, what your character is experiencing.

In these exercises you may choose an objective and a basic situation. Working with a second actor, you inform your colleague of your relationship, if any, to each other and the location of the action. Your acting partner should not have any additional information. You should determine your basic situation, your objectives, and the kind of human being you are. Beyond that you should make every effort not to structure the improvisation. For example, an actor may tell his colleague that the two have never met before and that they are inside an elevator. Once the improvisation is under way, the first actor must convey that the elevator has been trapped between floors. The first actor realizes that the stopping of the elevator is not a freak accident but an attempt to kill him; enemies have planned to have him bombed in the stalled elevator. The first actor must convey this to the other elevator passenger and enlist his help in an effort to get out of the stalled elevator before the time bomb explodes. Since gibberish is the only language between the actors, the two are forced to use their faces and bodies to communicate their needs. Usually, these exercises result in the actors' employing a heightened vitality and a vastly improved body language to communicate to each other and, hence, to the audience.

Here are some examples:

1. A door is thrown open, and a man is hurtled through it to the

floor. Following him into the room is another man who by his commanding presence and stentorian tones reveal that he is master of the situation. Slapping and manhandling the other man he is, we soon determine, an officer of a totalitarian government and is interrogating a political prisoner. The body language, faces, and vocal inflection of the two men make clear the factors involved in the situation.

2. Two girls are on a picnic in the country. It is night and they are roasting hot dogs over a fire. One girl has binoculars. While looking at the sky she thinks she sees something unusual. She tries to make the other girl see what she thinks is an unidentified flying object. The other girl at first is not convinced, but soon the audience can tell by the actions of the girls that the UFO is landing nearby. Frightened, the two girls run for their lives.

3. Kay is watching television when her girlfriend, Linda, stops by on her way home from a shopping trip. Linda is carrying two packages with her and presents one, a surprise gift, to Kay. Kay, delighted, opens the gift and discovers it's a beautiful hat. Stunned, Linda realizes that she has given Kay the wrong gift; she had intended to give her a much less expensive cloth scarf in the other package. She is about to explain the error when she sees how delighted Kay is with the gift and decides not to tell her of the mistake.

4. A fairy-tale quality prevails in this gibberish exercise which has a comedic sense to it. A "Prince Charming" and an "Ugly Witch" are the two characters. The Witch, riding her broom, swoops down on the Prince Charming. She has the ability to freeze the man in his actions whenever she thrusts her arm forward and speaks gibberish commands. Finally, through action and sounds, the Witch convinces Prince Charming that if he kisses her she will be transformed into a beautiful princess. Even though Prince Charming is repelled, he forces himself to kiss the Ugly Witch, hoping that she will turn beautiful. Unfortunately, the kiss doesn't produce the desired results.

ZEITGEIST

This exercise will assist you in developing the tool of memory of emotion. Since this exercise is very difficult, it should be used only by students in intermediate or advanced stages of training.

There is no effective English translation of the word, "Zeitgeist," a German word that describes a state of being. Yet this word defines a condition that can be of major importance in your acting development. Roughly translated, "Zeit" means "time" and "geist" means "spirit" but together the words imply a moment of great import in the actor's personal life, a "turning point," when his objectives were perhaps altered or clarified, a moment which has had considerable significance in his development as a human being.

This exercise will require several days of preparation on your part. You must search your mind for an experience which could properly be classified as a "Zeitgeist." Probably you will consider an event which is of such personal, relevatory nature that you reject it immediately. If this experience is not of a specific sexual nature, it is probably the most ideal "Zeitgeist" that you could choose. Once having recalled this "turning point" in your life, you should attempt to recall in detail all of the incidents that led up to the experience, and all the circumstances that surrounded the event. As much as possible, you should attempt to capture, once again, the enjoyment or suffering and its effect upon your judgments or feeling.

Once you have determined what constituted your "Zeitgeist," you should set up an improvisational situation in which all the factors surrounding this "turning point" are recaptured and re-experienced. You may enlist the aid of other actors to play individuals who are involved in the "Zeitgeist" experience with you. You should attempt as much as possible to recreate the environment and the circumstances that led up to and through the "Zeitgeist." It may be necessary for you to repeat the exercise many times before it is truly re-experienced. Finally, with the assistance of your acting colleagues, you are to re-experience this "Zeitgeist" before all the members of the workshop. This appearance before fellow actors is an essential part of the exercise since it forces you to be vulnerable before your peers. To no longer fear the revelation of one's weaknesses and one's innermost fears and doubts is to be liberated. Immediately you obtain a new-found freedom as an actor that inevitably leads you to become a finer artist.

Here are two examples of "Zeitgeists":

1. A young man whose father is a prominent attorney was attending a major university. On weekends he would join college buddies at a local bar where they would spend the evening drinking. One evening a middle-aged man joined them for drinks. He was not very well-educated. The young man and his buddies decided to make fun of the man. Taking him for a joyride through a remote area of the university campus, on an impulse they pushed the man out of their car, rolled him, and took his money. Shortly afterwards the young man was picked up by the police and accused of the theft. The young actor re-created the moment in jail when he is confronted by his father and must confess what he has done. To be sure, this was an excellent "Zeitgeist" experience for the young actor, and a decisive moment when he had to face up to his irresponsible actions and his failure to behave humanely.
2. A young man and his wife decided to have their baby by natural birth. Moreover, with the consent of their doctor, the man was to assist in the birth. The joy of bringing a life into the world and the sharing of a sublime and almost magical experience certainly constituted a "Zeitgeist." The actor re-experienced this moment preceding, during, and immediately following the birth of their child.

For the "Zeitgeist" exercises to achieve maximum effectiveness, it is important that the director and observing actors avoid making any ethical or moral value judgements. Any discussion of the actor's personal experience on the basis of its moral or social character is to be avoided. Instead the observer evaluates the "Zeitgeist" with these criteria:

1. Was the Zeitgeist recalled in its entirety?
2. Was the environment recaptured as much as possible?
3. Was the progression of emotional experiencing honest?
4. Did each progressive action grow out of an impelling need?

CHAPTER 4

CHEKOVIANS

Before undertaking the complexities of acting in a scene, an actor may learn some of the processes of rehearsing by working on some relatively uncomplicated "Chekovians." Chekovians are brief sequences of dialogue written so that they may be interpreted in many different ways depending on the wishes of the actors. The lines in these Chekovians have been intentionally selected to be as neutral as possible; they are completely unrevealing as to the kind of person who is saying them. Nothing in the lines particularly suggests anything about the physical, emotional, and intellectual qualities of the speakers. In the performance, if any sense of the character is communicated to the audience, it must be that the characterization was supplied by the actor and not by the author.

The participating actors decide for themselves where the "Chekovian" is taking place, what prior circumstances are relevant to the action, and what, if any, relationship there is between the participating characters. Without digression from the written lines and without the help of additional dialogue, the actors must make clear to the audience where the action is taking place, what is the relationship of the characters, and what is the basic premise of the scene. In developing the "Chekovian," the actors should ask themselves:

1. What is my character's objective?
2. What and how do I feel about my environment?
3. What activities should I employ to illuminate my character and his objective?

4. What is my relationship, if any, to the other characters in the action?

When the actors have done the "Chekovian" so that the audience understands where the action is taking place, what, if any, relationship there is between the characters, and what is the basic premise of the scene, then the teacher-director may choose to have the actors continue the exercise as an improvisation.

EXERCISES

CHEKOVIAN 1

This involves two characters. The actors choose their own location, time, prior circumstances, and relationship. These structured lines may be used, if so desired, at the beginning of an improvisation.

One

What took you so long?

Two

It's a long trip.

One

You look tired.

Two

I know. It hasn't been easy.

One

Were you so much in love?

Two

I thought so.

One

What about your loyalties to us?

Two

Don't worry. Everything's okay.

CHEKOVIAN 2

This involves two characters. The actors choose their own location, time, prior circumstances, and relationship. If so desired, these structured lines may be used as the beginning of an improvisation.

One

Hey! Am I glad to see you.

Two

I expect you're pretty surprised.

One

I hadn't expected to see you for a long time.

Two

Does that mean you haven't planned for me?

One

Oh . . . you'll fit in just beautifully.

Two

You haven't changed a bit, have you?

CHEKOVIAN 3

This involves two characters. The actors choose their own location, time, and relationship. They are looking off-stage or off-camera at one or more people who have just left as the action begins. If so desired, these structured lines may be used as the beginning of an improvisation.

One

What was that all about?

Two

Nothing . . . ask them if they want to know.

One

Why are you being so evasive?

Two

I'm not being evasive.

One

Something's going on . . . It isn't just my imagination.

Two

Nonsense! Look! I've got to go . . .

CHEKOVIAN 4

This involves four characters. The locale, time, and the relationship between the characters are of the actors' own choosing. If so desired, these structured lines may be used at the beginning of an improvisation.

One

Is everything going all right?

Two

You might say that.

Three

Why don't we all settle down and take it easy?

Four

That sounds like a good idea to me.

One

I'm willing to try anything. Anybody got a cigarette?

Two

Talk's cheap.

Three

Let's go get a beer or something.

Four

That's a cop-out.

CHEKOVIAN 5

This involves two characters. The locale, time, and the relationship between the characters are of the actor's own choosing. If so desired, these structured lines may be used at the beginning of an improvisation.

One

Hi.

Two

Hello.

One

What to go somewhere?

Two

Maybe.

One

You're looking well.

Two

Think so. Thanks.

One

What's new with you?

Two

What do you think?

CHEKOVIAN 6

This involves two characters. The locale, time, and the relationship between the characters are of the actor's own choosing. If so desired, these structured lines may be used at the beginning of an improvisation.

One

Hello!

Two

Hello!

One

Well!

Two

Well, what?

One

How are things?

Two

Just about as usual.

One

I didn't expect to find you here.

Two

Sure tells us something about each other, doesn't it?

One

What's that supposed to mean?

Two

Oh! Come on!

CHEKOVIAN 7

This involves two characters. The locale, time, and the relationship between the characters are of the actors' own choosing. If so desired, these structured lines may be used at the beginning of an improvisation.

One

Oh! I wasn't expecting you.

Two

That's okay. Is it all right if I sit down?

One

Why . . . sure! Tell me . . . is there some special reason for your coming here?

Two

Hmmm—your cordiality is about as cold as this place. Isn't there any heat?

One

Pardon me . . . I didn't mean to be "cold." I was just a little surprised.

Two

That's all right. The important thing right now is where is *it* hidden?

CHAPTER 5

IMPROVISATIONS

Although most actors are familiar with the use of improvisation, it may very well be the least understood acting tool employed by performers. Improvisations have often been a kind of "game" in which the actor has only a dim notion of its purpose. To be effective, improvisation should reveal to you some of the specific tools that you should employ in creating a believable character. When properly understood and used, improvisation can be a most helpful device in opening up areas of your psyche and freeing you from some of the emotional blocks that may weaken your effectiveness.

Improvisation reveals that you should respect your intuitions. You discover that there is a part of your mental processes that responds correctly to the moment without recourse to conscious reasoning. This innate, instinctive part of you, which comes from the unconscious, knows how to deal with the moment without intellectual perception. Actors must learn to trust these intuitions and not attempt to consciously manipulate a sequence. It is essential that you try not to guide the moment; you must permit the moment to emerge naturally, free from the ego-censor within yourself.

The joy of experiencing a successful improvisation is that it reveals to you how much you can trust your intuitions to lead you to make the right choices in creating a role. You will learn to permit each moment of the exercise to go in whatever direction it wishes. It will seem as though the character in the actions will have a mind of its own and dictate its wishes.

Actors with incorrect working methods often fail to trust their intuitions. They want to analyze their responses to a given situation; thinking that if they intellectually evaluate their responses first, they won't make a mistake. It is a natural inclination to assume that employing intelligence in this way will help the actor. Unfortunately, the very results the actor wishes to achieve will be mitigated by such working methods. This trust of the intellectual process and rejection of the intuitive process is a result of childhood training. By the time a person is six or seven years old his behavior is shaped not by what he wants or thinks he needs but on the basis of what he thinks will receive approval from the authority figures in his life. While this is a prerequisite for being accepted by one's peers, it is harmful to the creativity of the actor. Consequently, an actor must relearn to trust the intuitive part of himself that lies within his unconscious.

Before beginning an improvisation, you should know what are your environmental circumstances, the locale of the action, the basic situation that has brought about the conditions existing at the beginning of the action, your relationship to the characters you will encounter in the improvisation, and your objective as a character. Once the action begins, you as the character set out to achieve your character's objective. In the course of activities that transpire while you are attempting to achieve your objective, you may encounter various obstacles, interact with other characters whose objectives may be sympathetic or in opposition to yours, and experience feelings that are sometimes transitory and sometimes lengthy. You should not set out to consciously experience emotions. Emotional feelings are a result of the obstacles, events, and different kinds of relationships with other people that take place during the action. Working in an improvisation is similar to life, as one is constantly in a state of either minor or major "problem-solving." Since in life we rarely know what are the objectives of the other individuals we encounter, the same conditions should prevail in an improvisation. In the improvisations that follow, you and your fellow actors are given your objectives *separately* from each other so that there can be *no pre-planning* of your interaction. As in life, you and the other characters in the improvisation may find you share objectives or you may find that their different objectives bring them into conflict with you and your objectives. Again, as in life, the character's objectives may have to be revised or reshaped in accordance with their conflict of interest.

Having been given an objective, you should maintain a steady progress toward the achieving of that objective so long as the objective is being pursued in a natural way. For example, you may have as your objective the buying of a new shirt. If, on your way to the store, you become involved in an automobile accident, it is natural that your objective shall change. No longer is it important whether you get your shirt or not. Someone else may be hurt or you may be hurt, and there may be legal problems as a result of the accident. In any event, it is probable that your objective has changed from buying a shirt to some other more serious objective that may have long-range complications. In an improvisation when you, as your character, find it is no longer tenable to maintain a certain objective, you should not be afraid to change your objective.

If an improvisation is to be beneficial to you, you must painstakingly avoid falling into the trap of "playwriting." At no time prior to or during an improvisation should you consciously attempt to control the shape or direction of the exercise. You should not think of improvisations as "scenes" that must be dramatically effective. Stop thinking "scene." An improvisation may not be very effective as a "scene" and yet be valuable to you if it teaches you to trust your intuitions and reveals to you how to work organically from moment-to-moment concerning yourself only with each moment-in-time, and if it leads you to work truthfully without censorship or editing.

It is immediately evident when an actor is not working in an improvisation correctly. First, the patent dishonesty of his work will be apparent. Secondly, his behavior is likely to be "actorish" rather than human. Thirdly, the actor will tend to verbalize his situation rather than deal with it in a natural, active way. Verbalizing is that almost compulsive need to talk endlessly whether the words are pertinent or not to the character's objectives and situation. Additionally, actors manipulating their situations rather than working organically within them will fear silence. In real-life situations when we are confronted with problems that do not offer up immediate solutions, we frequently are stumped for words. We respond with silence until we have thought of some way to deal with the problem. The same kind of response should prevail in an improvisation. The actor who is working incorrectly will invariably find it necessary to fill the silence with words regardless of their relevance or even their appropriateness to the moment.

In working in an improvisation, you should concern yourself with these questions:

1. Am I honest? Am I working without censoring, editing, or manipulating?
2. Am I using my personal emotional resources truthfully?
3. Am I concentrating? Are my energies focused? Am I really dealing with my objectives as a character?
4. Am I really relating to my environment? Are the conditions of the environment influencing me as they would if I were truly in such an environment?
5. Am I dealing with each moment-in-time just as I would have to deal with each individual moment-in-time in life?
6. Am I really listening to the other people in the exercise? Am I observing their physical response to the moment? As in life, am I making value judgments on the basis of their body actions and reactions?
7. Am I constantly making a series of adaptations on the basis of new information and changing circumstances within the exercise?

In the course of an improvisation, the actor as a character will confront various obstacles and events, will find himself interrelating with other people, and dealing with problems that occur. All of this results in experiencing feelings that are sometimes transitory and sometimes lengthy. However, the actor, as the character, did not set out to consciously experience these emotions. These emotions are a natural response to the obstacles, events, and different relating experiences to people that have taken place. When a man sets out to go to his daily job it is not his goal to be either happy or unhappy. The man's immediate objective is to go to his work. The individual doesn't think of being happy or unhappy; he is not consciously thinking of what his emotions might be. Instead, he is concerned with getting to his place of work so that he can do specific tasks. However, while on his way to work, he may have an uncomfortable ride on the bus. Perhaps the vehicle was crowded so that he had to stand all the way downtown. He didn't want to be irritable; it was the inevitable result of his unpleasant ride. As soon as he entered the office he was confronted by his supervisor who asked, "Why didn't you finish the job last night before leaving for home?" That's all the person needed to bring his irritation out into the open. "Damn it! I did the job," the man replied. Now he is unhappy and angry. Did he plan to feel this way? No. A person doesn't plan to be unhappy. A person doesn't plan to experience that kind of emotion; it is a result of the events that have transpired. Acting, then, should be as reflective of life. An actor does not concern himself with emotion; it is a result of the events that take place within his dramatic situation.

A teacher-director makes best use of improvisation when he matches the exercise with the kind of emotional-sensory resources he assumes the actor possesses. He is helping develop the actor's freedom when the performer is triggered by the inherent elements of the improvisation and is forced to employ those emotions most characteristic of himself.

In evaluating the success of an improvisation, suggestions are useless if they are directed toward the actor's choice of actions. It is irrelevant what kind of choice-making the actor makes providing those choices are pertinent to the character's objectives and consistent with the actor's emotional and sensory resources. For an individual to tell an actor what he would have done in the same situation may be interesting but is hardly important to the actor's development.

HOW TO USE THE IMPROVISATION EXERCISES:

These improvisations are written so that you read only those portions that include necessary information for your participation. So that the improvisation may truly be spontaneous it is necessary and important that you *read only those portions pertaining to you.* The improvisation will inevitably fail if you read the information pertaining to other participating characters.

Everyone involved in the improvisation should read the first part of the exercise. It includes this information:

1. The characters who are involved in the improvisation.
2. The setting where the event is taking place.
3. The situation which includes events, prior information, and relationships that are pertinent to the knowledge of all the participants in the improvisation.

Following this portion which all those participating in the improvisation read, you will find the individual objectives of each participating actor. If you are playing the "first character" you will find your objective listed opposite the appropriate exercise number beginning on page 85. If you are playing the "second character" you will find your objective listed oppose the appropriate exercise number beginning on page 99. In those improvisations requiring a "third or fourth character" you will find their objectives listed opposite the appropriate exercise numbers beginning on page 113.

Read your character's objective only. Please do not read your acting partner's objective if you wish the improvisation to be effective. When you have completed the improvisation, you will find that you have experienced a number of sensations, impressions, and learning experiences that you will want to evaluate. At the end of the section on improvisations you will find a questionnaire. Answer this questionnaire after each improvisation you do; it will assist you in determining whether you are making progress in your improvisations as one of the tools for becoming a fine actor.

EXERCISE 1 (A YOUNG MAN AND A YOUNG WOMAN)

The Characters: A young man and a young woman.

The Setting: A hospital room in a large city. There are bouquets of flowers, a small table, a regulation hospital bed, a wheelchair, and a couple of straight-back chairs.

The Situation: A young man and a young woman, very much in love, have planned to be married. He has a promising career as an architect; she is in her final year of college where she has proven to be an outstanding student. On their way to church to be married, their automobile is involved in an accident in which both are injured. While injuries to the young man have been minor the young woman has suffered more serious injuries involving brain surgery. Now the girl is getting well and will be released from the hospital in another two weeks. However, the accident has caused the young man to feel that his carelessness was one of the reasons for the accident.

(PLEASE DO NOT READ YOUR ACTING PARTNER'S OBJECTIVE IF YOU WANT THE EXERCISE TO BE EFFECTIVE.)

EXERCISE 2 (A TEENAGE BOY, HIS MOTHER)

The Characters: A teenage boy; his mother.

The Setting: An abandoned-looking apartment in a ramshackle building that is located in the bohemian section of a large city.

The Situation: The young boy is sleeping in the apartment. The room is empty except for two mattresses and a few blankets strewn on the floor. The action begins as there is a knock at the door. When the boy awakens and goes to open the door, he is surprised to discover his mother standing on the threshold. She lives at least a thousand miles away from his present living quarters; he has not expected her.

EXERCISE 3 (A WOMAN IN HER MID-TWENTIES, HER SLIGHTLY YOUNGER BROTHER)

The Characters: A famous female singer with a leading musical group that is popular with young people; her brother.

The Setting: The shabby bedroom of a sleazy motel in a run-down section of a large city.

The Situation: For the past two years the girl has been a great popular success. She has many record hits and plays to huge audiences at her concerts all over the world. She is adulated by young people, and thus her hectic schedule has made it impossible for her to visit her family. Her family are simple, country people who love her very much; she, in turn, loves them. As the action begins, she is lying, half-asleep, on the bed in the shabby motel room.

EXERCISE 4 (A MIDDLE-AGED MAN, HIS SLIGHTLY YOUNGER WIFE)

The Characters: A husband and wife who are in their middle years.

The Setting: The pleasantly furnished lovely suburban home of an upper-middle-class family.

The Situation: The couple has been happily married for twenty-five years; they have two children who are now adults and beginning successful careers of their own. Recently the man has begun to drink heavily, and the wife has found herself nagging him. As the action begins, it is 2 A.M. and the man has not arrived home from a business meeting.

(PLEASE DO NOT READ YOUR ACTING PARTNER'S OBJECTIVE
IF YOU WANT THE EXERCISE TO BE EFFECTIVE)

EXERCISE 5 (YOUNG MAN, YOUNG WOMAN IN EARLY THIRTIES)

The Characters: A young man and woman in their early thirties.

The Setting: A park in a large city that has a merry-go-round for children.

The Situation: A young couple, formerly married to each other, has been divorced for a little more than a year. The wife gained custody of their only child, Wendy. The divorce was precipitated when the young woman discovered that her husband was having an affair with his secretary, Marilyn. It is Wendy's birthday and, as a gesture of good will, the divorced couple has gone to the park together to celebrate the occasion. During the action they sometimes watch their daughter Wendy who is riding on the merry-go-round.

EXERCISE 6 (A HUSBAND AND WIFE)

The Characters: A husband and wife.

The Setting: The visiting room of a city jail.

The Situation: A wife visits her husband in jail. He has been accused of a serious crime (to be decided in advance by the two actors involved in the exercise) and will soon be on trial. As the action begins, the wife is waiting for her husband to be brought into the visiting room.

(PLEASE DO NOT READ YOUR ACTING PARTNER'S OBJECTIVE IF YOU WANT THE EXERCISE TO BE EFFECTIVE)

EXERCISE 7 (A YOUNG MAN AND HIS FIANCÉE)

The Characters: A young man and his fiancée.

The Setting: The crowded terminal of the Las Vegas Airport.

The Situation: The couple has flown to Las Vegas to get married. Before going to the wedding chapel, they stop at one of the resort hotels for lunch. As they eat, the young man becomes serious and he confesses that he was once hospitalized for several months with a mental disorder. Seeing his girl's alarmed reaction, he quickly reassures her that his former illness is very much a part of the past and it is no threat to their present happiness or their future. The girl, however, becomes hysterical and tells the young man that she has to go to the ladies' room. When the girl does not return to the dining room to rejoin the young man, he goes to look for her. He learns that she has run out of the hotel and hailed a taxi. Surmising that she has gone to the airport, he calls a cab and hurries there. Arriving at the airport, he spies her in the crowded terminal as the action begins.

EXERCISE 8 (A YOUNG KIDNAPPER AND HIS YOUNG WOMAN CAPTIVE)

The Characters: A young man who is a kidnapper and the rich young woman who is his captive.

The Setting: A dingy, dark room furnished only with a table, two hard straight-back chairs, and a telephone.

The Situation: A kidnapper and the young woman he has kidnapped are holed-up in a room somewhere; they have been there for several hours. He is waiting for a telephone call from his confederate in the kidnapping. The call from his co-conspirator should be made within a few minutes after the action begins. (The director-teacher may serve as the voice on the telephone and may choose either to call, or not call the kidnapper.) The time is a little after 2 A.M., and the important telephone call is already overdue.

EXERCISE 9 (MIDDLE-AGED MAN AND YOUNG WOMAN)

The Characters: A middle-aged college professor and a girl student.

The Setting: A classroom of a small, famed Eastern college. It is late afternoon during the winter quarter.

The Situation: The college professor and the girl student have become very friendly, transcending the usual student-teacher relationship. Both are aware that their relationship may appear questionable in the eyes of the administration and the student body.

(PLEASE DO NOT READ YOUR ACTING PARTNER'S OBJECTIVE IF YOU WISH THE EXERCISE TO ENJOY MAXIMUM SUCCESS)

EXERCISE 10 (A YOUNG MAN AND A YOUNG WOMAN)

The Characters: A poor young man and a wealthy young woman.

The Setting: The nicely designed and furnished apartment of the young woman.

The Situation: A young man, poor and not very successful, meets a young woman whose family is wealthy. They start dating each other, fall in love, begin an affair. Last week the young woman disappeared without telling the young man that she was going to be away. He has been frantically calling her at the apartment ever since in the hope that she has returned. When he called her parents to inquire about her, they were cold in their response and said that they did not know where the girl might be. Finally, when he telephoned today, the young woman answered the phone. Before she can tell him anything, the young man hangs up and rushes to her apartment. He arrives as the action begins.

EXERCISE 11 (MAN AND WOMAN)

The Characters: A young man and his mother.

The Setting: A small studio apartment in a tenement section of a large city; it is mid-winter and late in the afternoon.

The Situation: The young man and his mother fight a never-ending struggle against abject poverty. The woman was a musical comedy performer in partnership with her now-deceased husband. When he died it soon became apparent that her career was over. To support her young son and herself, she took work as a cocktail waitress. As her son grew and her looks faded, the woman began drinking. Soon she was forced to make a meager living as a seamstress. She has become an alcoholic whose working capacity has greatly diminished. Now the two depend on the income from the young man's part-time job as a stock clerk. Ambitious, the young man is also attending college on a part-time basis. He works long, difficult hours and is frequently exhausted.

(FOR MAXIMUM SUCCESS, PLEASE DO NOT READ YOUR ACTING PARTNER'S OBJECTIVE.)

EXERCISE 12 (MAN AND WOMAN)

The Characters: A college student; his stepmother.

The Setting: The entrance way to a college campus; it is 11 P.M. on a school night.

The Situation: A student at school has called his stepmother asking her to pick him up. He was supposed to get a ride home much earlier in the evening. When he did not appear for dinner, his stepmother was quite concerned since her husband, the student's father, is out of town on business. The action begins with the arrival of the stepmother's automobile at the college campus gate.

EXERCISE 13 (MAN AND WOMAN)

The Characters: A mother and her son.

The Setting: The young man's apartment in Hollywood. It is small, neat, attractively furnished; it is obvious that the young man has taste and is interested in the arts.

The Situation: The young man is the product of his mother and father's premarital relations. Forced into a marriage neither wanted by the eminent birth of the boy, the very young couple soon divorced. The father remarried and has two children by his second marriage. The young man's mother, who raised the son, has never remarried but has had many men friends. Always indulging in her own pleasures and frequently promiscuous, she neglected her son. Finally, when he reached sixteen, the boy was sent to live with the father. This living situation was intolerable, and the boy escaped into the military service. He has not seen his mother for nine years. The action begins when the son, answering a knock at his door, is surprised to see his mother after all this time.

EXERCISE 14 (MAN AND WOMAN)

The Characters: A husband and wife.

The Setting: The rear garden of the couple's pleasant suburban home.

The Situation: While your marriage has been characterized as a good one, it has not been filled with great happiness. To a considerable degree you both have pursued your own interests and shared only those experiences necessary to maintain the marriage. You have two children—a boy who is now in his first year of college away from home and a daughter who is only fifteen. The action takes place as the husband emerges from the house to join his wife who is working in the garden.

(FOR MAXIMUM SUCCESS, PLEASE DO NOT READ YOUR ACTING PARTNER'S OBJECTIVE.)

EXERCISE 15 (MAN AND WOMAN)

The Characters: A husband and wife.

The Setting: Their bedroom; the couple is asleep.

The Situation: It is night and the couple has been sleeping. The wife is eight months' pregnant. At four in the morning the husband awakens to discover his wife also awake, tossing and turning in bed. Her agitation is sufficient to concern him.

EXERCISE 16 (MAN AND WOMAN)

The Characters: A husband and wife.

The Setting: The couple's home in a metropolitan city.

The Situation: A very happily married couple, the husband and wife first met in South America where the man, a U.S. citizen, was helping organize the law enforcement organization of a large city. The woman was the daughter of a prominent South American businessman. Falling in love, the two eloped. After coming to the United States with her husband, the woman became a naturalized citizen. Since then the career of the husband has steadily climbed, and he has become a nationally known expert in criminology. Today the United States government has offered him a key position with the highly secret Central Intelligence Agency. It seems a wonderful advancement for the couple with a large increase in income; it puts the man in the highest echelons of government. Thrilled at the prospects of the new job, the husband has called home to tell his wife of this major promotion. The action begins as the husband arrives home.

EXERCISE 17 (MAN AND WOMAN)

The Characters: A husband and wife.

The Setting: The living room of a middle-income family. It is approximately 2 o'clock in the morning.

The Situation: The husband and wife have been married for ten years and have three children. The wife, before her marriage, was pursuing a career in show business that she gave up with the birth of the first child. This is the second marriage for the man, who is divorced from his first wife.

(FOR MAXIMUM SUCCESS, PLEASE DO NOT READ YOUR ACTING PARTNER'S OBJECTIVE.)

EXERCISE 18 (MAN AND WOMAN)

The Characters: A doctor and his wife.

The Setting: A hotel bedroom at a fashion resort.

The Situation: The couple has been married for five years. They are very much in love. For some reason that may be determined by the actors involved before the improvisation begins, she has become addicted to morphine. Against his better judgment, the doctor has been providing his wife with the needed drugs. They are on vacation and staying at a resort hotel in the mountains.

EXERCISE 19 (MAN AND WOMAN)

The Characters: A young woman preacher of an evangelistic church and her younger brother.

The Setting: The living room and the boy's bedroom of the small wooden-framed house belonging to the woman preacher.

The Situation: Earlier this evening, the sister and her brother had an argument regarding attendance at religious meetings. The woman told her younger brother that he could only achieve salvation through her, and he replied that she was a hypocrite. He refused to attend the prayer meeting, and the sister stamped off in a fury. As the action begins, the sister is returning to the home she shares with her younger brother.

EXERCISE 20 (MAN AND WOMAN)

The Characters: A young man and a young woman.

The Setting: The young couple's small, attractive apartment on the tenth floor of a large apartment house in New York.

The Situation: The young couple is struggling with their respective careers. She is a young actress of considerable promise who studies at an acting workshop during the day and works as a waitress from 6 P.M. to 2

A.M. to provide finances for the couple. He is doing graduate work at Columbia University and works weekends in a shoe store. Although they have discussed marriage, the two have agreed that it would not be compatible with their career objectives, their financial status, and their current life-styles. They do love each other and are faithful to each other. As the action begins, the girl enters the apartment at 3 A.M. to discover the young man standing on the sill of an open window ten floors above the concrete sidewalk. He appears to be in a state of shock.

(FOR MAXIMUM SUCCESS, PLEASE DO NOT READ YOUR ACTING PARTNER'S OBJECTIVE.)

EXERCISE 21 (MAN AND WOMAN)

The Characters: A man and a woman.

The Setting: The living room of her home.

The Situation: The man and woman are having a love affair. He is married, and his wife spends about half of each year in another part of the country with her parents. The man has three children whom he loves deeply. It is about one and a half weeks before the husband's wife is supposed to return from her parents' home.

EXERCISE 22 (MAN AND WOMAN)

The Characters: A husband and wife.

The Setting: The street outside a mental hospital and the interior of a car belonging to the married couple. Once the action begins it is possible that the automobile will sometimes be in motion depending on the choices made by the driver.

The Situation: The husband and wife have been married for several years; both of them have enjoyed considerable success. He is a successful fashion model who has appeared in many television commercials and in print advertisements in all the national magazines. She is a part-time actress who aspires to a full-time career. Their life together has been one of too many parties, too much booze, and spurts of hard work. Bad things have existed in their lives too. He would prefer pursuing a career as a writer but has been unwilling to give up the lucrative income he makes as a model to concentrate on writing. Furthermore, he is estranged from his parents who live in Europe; they have rejected his life-style and, even more importantly, his marriage to his wife. The fact that she has been unable to get her acting career to develop successfully has also been a problem for the couple. He had a nervous breakdown and has been in the sanitarium for the past six months. The action begins upon his release from the hospital and his first meeting with his wife.

(FOR MAXIMUM SUCCESS, PLEASE DO NOT READ YOUR ACTING PARTNER'S OBJECTIVE.)

EXERCISE 23 (MAN AND WOMAN)

The Characters: A hopeless alcoholic; a woman unknown to him.

The Setting: A jail cell.

The Situation: The man has been a known alcoholic for more than fifteen years. Often in jail on vagrancy charges, the man has a history of mental blackouts during which he can remember little or nothing of what has taken place. Now the man finds himself jailed on kidnapping charges. For some reason unknown to the prisoner, who is soon to go on trial, a woman is brought into the jail cell to talk to him. The action begins with the arrival of the woman.

EXERCISE 24 (TWO YOUNG MEN)

The Characters: Two men in their early twenties.

The Setting: The living room of a luxurious ski lodge. It is mid-winter and quite cold outside.

The Situation: The two men have been friends since childhood, but as they grew older their lives took different paths. One stayed in Callaway, Kentucky, and followed his father's life's work of coal mining. The other is the son of the owner of a high-tech company which manufactures computer chips and computer software; this company is located in California. The Kentuckian is bound to the life of a coal miner while the Californian has become a senior vice president of the company his father heads. Each year the affluent young Californian, along with his father, has flown his Kentucky friend out to the coast for a week of skiing in the Sierras. This year the three men have enjoyed the week of skiing until yesterday when the father of the affluent Californian suffered a fatal skiing accident when he skied off a cliff in an area outside the patrolled ski boundaries.

EXERCISE 25 (TWO MEN)

The Characters: A college student; a young police officer.

The Setting: The college student's automobile and the street.

The Situation: A young man in his second year of college is on his way home from a party. As he drives down the street of the college town where he lives, he notices the red light on a police car flashing behind him, signalling him to stop. The action begins as he stops his car and the police officer walks from his patrol car to the student's car.

(FOR MAXIMUM SUCCESS, PLEASE DO NOT READ YOUR ACTING PARTNER'S OBJECTIVE.)

EXERCISE 26 (TWO MEN)

The Characters: Two brothers.

The Setting: The office of the younger brother in a manufacturing plant. The time is 11 P.M.

The Situation: A successful middle-sized family business is operated by an old man and his two sons. Manufacturing men's pants, the firm is still nominally headed by the father although the two sons handle the day-to-day business. Neither of the sons receive salaries commensurate with their positions or their responsibilities. Certainly, they don't make as large salaries as the company's success warrants. The father has never disclosed the contents of his will, and the two sons often wonder whether one is favored over the other. The rivalry between the two brothers has not been restricted to dominance in the business. The younger brother courted Mary, and the couple was seriously interested in each other until the older brother met the girl. After a series of dates, the older brother won Mary away from the younger brother. As the action of the improvisation begins, the younger brother has returned late at night to the combination office-factory. As the company's accountant, he is working on the financial ledger. After a few moments he is surprised when he is unexpectedly joined by the older brother who has been bar-hopping.

EXERCISE 27 (TWO MEN)

The Characters: A young boxer and his older brother.

The Setting: A dressing room at a boxing arena.

The Situation: A young fighter is about to go into the ring for the sixth in a series of boxing matches that have led toward the young boxer's success in the ring. The progress of the young fighter indicates that he has a good chance of becoming a champion. Acting as his manager is his older brother, a former boxer who once had a promising career as a fighter. When something went wrong with the older brother's career, his aspirations for the championship were not realized. The older brother has become his younger brother's manager. With only ten minutes left before the start of the bout, the older brother has cleared the dressing room of well-wishers and sports fans. The action begins as he closes the door, leaving the dressing room to himself and his brother.

EXERCISE 28 (TWO MEN)

The Characters: A grizzled old man; a teenage boy.

The Setting: A tiny shack on a ranch somewhere in the Southwest. Approximately 500 feet from the farmhouse, the shack houses livestock feed, harnesses, and small farm supplies. It is early morning in winter with the sun still below the horizon and the sky just beginning to lighten.

The Situation: The teenage boy crosses the yard and enters the shack. Still half-asleep, he is carrying a bucket that he plans to fill with feed. Inside the shack he almost stumbles over the sleeping figure of the old man. Neither individual knows the other.

EXERCISE 29 (TWO MEN)

The Characters: An eighteen-year-old man and his twenty-two-year-old brother.

The Setting: A bedroom shared by the two brothers in their family home.

The Situation: Coming home from a party, the eighteen-year-old is surprised to discover his brother packing some clothes and other belongings into a suitcase; his record player is locked up and ready for moving. None of the other members of the family are home since they have gone on a weekend holiday. The older brother recently moved into a fraternity house at the latest of several successive colleges he has attended, and the younger brother did not expect his brother to be at the family home. Neither brother has been very close to each other during the last couple of years.

EXERCISE 30 (TWO MEN)

The Characters: Two combat medics.

The Setting: A barren, isolated hill, relatively unprotected, in the middle of a combat area.

The Situation: Both men are medics in the same combat unit. During a harsh skirmish Medic #1 has been severely injured with his left leg in particular pain. Medic #2 is uninjured. The two men have been cut off from their unit and, to the best of their knowledge, may be surrounded by enemy troops. Nightfall is eminent, and it is very cold. Although both men are dedicated medics, they are not good friends.

(FOR MAXIMUM SUCCESS, PLEASE DO NOT READ YOUR ACTING PARTNER'S OBJECTIVE.)

EXERCISE 31 (TWO MEN)

The Characters: A motion picture producer; his star who is a young man making his first film.

The Setting: The office of the film producer; it is late in the afternoon.

The Situation: As the action begins, a meeting is about to take place between the producer and a fledgling young actor who has been given a major role in the producer's current film, A LONELY PEACE. It is 7 P.M. after a long and particularly trying day of shooting. The action begins as the young actor, exhausted after the day's turbulent shooting, enters the producer's office.

EXERCISE 32 (TWO MEN)

The Characters: A father and his son.

The Setting: The strongly masculine study of a successful attorney; the room reveals the personality of its chief inhabitant. It is the Christmas holiday season.

The Situation: The son arrives home from college to spend the Christmas holidays with his family. He is attending a university where he is studying pre-law. His father has not yet seen him when the action begins. Culturally oriented, the boy has studied music, art, and drama as well as the law. His musical talents, as those of his father before him, have been considerable.

EXERCISE 33 (TWO MEN)

The Characters: An old man; a young man.

The Setting: The back booth of a small bar-restaurant in a large city.

The Situation: The old man, dressed prosperously, is waiting for a young man whom he has not seen before but with whom he has talked on the telephone. The young man was reached by phone when the old man read an advertisement in the "Want Ads" of the newspaper in which the young man was seeking work as an "adventurer." The action begins a few moments before the arrival of the young man; the old man is seated in the booth.

(FOR MAXIMUM SUCCESS, PLEASE DO NOT READ YOUR ACTING PARTNER'S OBJECTIVE.)

EXERCISE 34 (TWO WOMEN)

The Characters: A youthful mother and her sixteen-year-old daughter.

The Setting: The living room of a modern apartment. Dinner is over, and the two women are having coffee in the living room.

The Situation: Widowed, the mother lives with her daughter. Although she has a small insurance payment every month, the woman works to help support her daughter and herself. The mother and daughter are very close and love each other very much. They are discussing a ski trip that the daughter will be taking this weekend with two of her girlfriends. The daughter is sixteen; this will be the first time she has been away from home overnight without adult supervision. The mother has reluctantly agreed to the trip.

(FOR MAXIMUM SUCCESS, PLEASE DO NOT READ YOUR ACTING PARTNER'S OBJECTIVE.)

EXERCISE 35 (TWO WOMEN)

The Characters: A mother and her teenage daughter.

The Setting: On the beach at the seashore.

The Situation: They are at an outing together on a bright, pleasant summer day. They have found a private spot of beach and are settling down as the action begins. The woman's husband, who is the teenager's father, died three years ago. Shortly after his death the child was put into a foster home; it is rare that the parent and child visit each other.

EXERCISE 36 (SEVERAL PEOPLE)

The Characters: Two young men and possibly a third person, of either sex, who is the Dean of students at a college. The person who is playing the Dean of students may choose either to participate or not participate in the exercise. If this actor does join the two men in the improvisation, it should be done in the latter part of the exercise.

The Setting: The reception room and possibly the private office of the Dean of students at a small college on the Eastern seaboard. It is late afternoon in May as the action commences.

The Situation: A young male student, Ron, has drowned in a freak accident at the seashore near the college. He was found partly buried in the sand. Further up the beach a number of whisky and beer bottles have been found. The local police department is investigating the strange case and suspects foul play. As the action begins, two students arrive separately, but simultaneously at the Dean's office. They have been called by the Dean of students who wants to know more about the drowning of the student, Ron.

(FOR MAXIMUM SUCCESS, PLEASE DO NOT READ YOUR ACTING PARTNER'S OBJECTIVE.)

EXERCISE 37 (SEVERAL PEOPLE)

The Characters: A neophyte actress; her mother; her director.

The Setting: Onstage during a rehearsal break; the show is in rehearsal preparing for an off-Broadway production.

The Situation: During a break from a long rehearsal for a new show to open in an off-Broadway theater, the young actress and the director are having a quiet discussion over coffee. Other members of the cast have stepped out of the theater to have a cigarette. As the action begins, the actress's mother makes a surprise visit to the theater and joins the talking couple.

EXERCISE 38 (SEVERAL PEOPLE)

The Characters: A South American businessman; his wife; a second man previously unknown to the husband and wife.

The Setting: The dark living room of the couple's home.

The Situation: The action begins with the arrival home of the couple at midnight. As they entered the darkened living room, they are confronted by an unknown man who is carrying a gun.

EXERCISE 39 (SEVERAL PEOPLE)

The Characters: A black man; his Caucasian wife; a Caucasian nurse.

The Setting: The reception room of a hospital in the deep south.

The Situation: A woman, obviously in the early stages of labor, has just arrived at the hospital. She is accompanied by her husband, a black man.

(FOR MAXIMUM SUCCESS, PLEASE DO NOT READ YOUR ACTING PARTNER'S OBJECTIVE.)

EXERCISE 40 (SEVERAL PEOPLE)

The Characters: A husband; his wife; a stranger unknown to the couple.

The Setting: The living room of the couple just prior to a cocktail party.

The Situation: Tonight the couple is giving an important cocktail party dinner for a group of people who are both friends and influential business associates. On this particular occasion the husband is supposed to arrive home by 5:30 since the party is to start at 7:30. The time is already 6:45 and for some reason the husband has not arrived home. The action begins a few seconds before the late arrival of the husband.

(FOR MAXIMUM SUCCESS, PLEASE DO NOT READ YOUR ACTING PARTNER'S OBJECTIVE.)

EXERCISE 41 (SEVERAL PEOPLE)

The Characters: Two young men; two young women.

The Setting: A lonely country road late at night.

The Situation: It is a warm and soft spring evening. The raucous sound of crickets can be heard in the background. The action begins as a car careens to a stop, its headlights picking out the writhing body of a person whom the car has just hit. The person is moaning and unconscious. The couples have been driving home from a play rehearsal. In spite of the other passengers' protests, the driver of the car has insisted to his friends that they join him in a country drive to relax after a strenuous rehearsal. After a while they all began having fun, and while everyone sang the driver weaved the car back and forth on the country road when suddenly the headlights picked up the figure of someone walking alongside the country road. The driver swerved the car frantically, but it was too late. A thud is heard, followed by a cry. As the action begins, the car's occupants rush toward the body of the man lying on the road.

EXERCISE 42 (TWO PEOPLE, EITHER SEX)

The Characters: A teacher; a parent.

The Setting: An empty classroom late in the afternoon after the students have gone home.

The Situation: The teacher is employed by a special school for emotionally disturbed children. It is late afternoon when the action begins with the entrance of a parent. The teacher knows immediately that the parent is visiting the school to discuss the parent's ten-year-old boy.

EXERCISE 43 (TWO PEOPLE, EITHER SEX)

The Characters: Two people who are strangers to each other.

The Setting: A large living room or lobby in what appears to be a middle-class rooming house. The decor does not suggest any specific period, but it is evident that the furnishings are not contemporary. There are windows that open out to a garden that is overgrown and heavily veiled by bushes. The doors leading outdoors can be opened, but have never been opened by the room's inhabitants. A stairway leads into the room, and it is down this part of the building that one of the two people makes his entrance.

The Situation: The individual making his entrance down the stairs cannot remember any prior action; all he recalls is his name and those friends and relatives who have been closest to him in the past. He seems to be suffering from amnesia and cannot remember where he is or what he has been doing for the last several days. The person who is sitting in the room is a stranger to him. During the course of the action, neither of them for some reason unknown to the participants dares to leave the house through the outside entrance.

(FOR MAXIMUM SUCCESS, PLEASE DO NOT READ YOUR ACTING PARTNER'S OBJECTIVE.)

EXERCISE 44 (TWO PEOPLE, EITHER SEX)

The Characters: An adult supervisor; a juvenile delinquent.

The Setting: The interior of an automobile and the desolate roadway that leads to a detention home for delinquents. It is late at night and very cold.

The Situation: While driving back to the detention home, the supervisor picks out a figure in the car's headlights; he is trudging beside the road. There are deep ditches on both sides of the road so that the walking person cannot flee far. Jamming on the brakes, the car grinds to a halt and the action begins as the supervisor runs toward the inmate who is trying to escape. During the preliminary action the supervisor succeeds in catching the inmate.

EXERCISE 45 (TWO PEOPLE, EITHER SEX)

The Characters: Two college students of the same sex who are approximately the same age.

The Setting: The dormitory room of the two college students; the action takes place following dinner in the college dining room.

The Situation: The two young people are new roommates at school. This is the seventh week of their first semester at this college; they have become good friends. During this period of time, they have gone shopping together on several occasions. During these excursions, Roommate #2 has witnessed Roommate #1 shoplift a traveling clock, a muffler, and a box of candy. Alarmed, Roommate #2 admonished Roommate #1 for these dangerous sprees. Roommate #1 replied simply that it was a "lark" and that the action would never be repeated.

FIRST CHARACTER

EXERCISE 1

The Young Man's Objectives: You have come to visit your girlfriend with some very real problems weighing heavily on your mind. You have learned from the doctors that the apparent recovery of your girl is not a true indication of her health. She will seem well for several months, but the surgery did not correct the damage to her brain. There is still excessive pressure upon her brain which after a period of time will result in the deterioration of her mental faculties. The doctors have told you that any great emotional stress or unusual excitement could result in speeding up this deterioration. In conferring with the doctors you have learned that no purpose will be achieved by informing the girl of her fate. Consequently, the state of her health has been kept from her. Therefore, you are faced with several problems: you want the girl to know that you truly love her; you have to decide for yourself whether you should marry her; and you realize that the excitement of a marriage would hasten her mental breakdown. From this group of facts, you choose your objective in the improvisation.

EXERCISE 2

The Teenage Boy's Objective: You left home after a particularly bitter altercation with your stepfather. Your mother was not present during this argument. Your real father disappeared when you were five years old, and he has not been seen since. You love your mother but despise your stepfather. Recently you discovered that your stepfather has sired an illegitimate child. You threatened to disclose this information to your mother. Very angry, your stepfather swore that he would kill you if you told your mother. Realizing how much you are hated by your stepfather, you have fled a thousand miles away from home and joined a group of runaway kids living together in this apartment. You have missed your mother but know that you must never go home. You are searching for love and purpose in your life.

EXERCISE 3

The Young Woman's Objective: Your recording-concert success has become a nightmare. Because you were under severe strain at the beginning of your career and involved in an accelerated series of activities, your manager gave you "pep" pills to keep you going. Soon you were addicted to pills that would either wake you up and keep you lively or put you to sleep so you could get much needed rest. Always strained to the breaking point, you went to a late night party one evening on the eighth floor of a hotel. High on pills, nerves stretched thin, you had a fight with your personal manager. In a burst of fury you struck out at him and pushed him through a plate glass window to his death. The people at the party, all of whom benefited from your successful career, hushed up the death, claiming it was an accident. Now these people control you professionally, economically, and spiritually. Although you sing songs of freedom and the uniqueness of the individual, your soul is literally possessed by these people. Needing a release from your burdens, you have gone on a "pill" trip for the last three days. Some time during the trip you ended up in this sleazy motel room.

EXERCISE 4 *The Husband's Objective*: You are fifty-four years old and experiencing the most anxiety-ridden period in your life since you were a teenager. Six months ago your corporation was absorbed by a conglomerate of companies and your services were no longer needed. You were given a substantial severance pay that is now running out. Every working day of the week you have been searching for another executive position, but you've found that corporations are reluctant to hire a man your age since it is costly in terms of retirement policies and other expense factors. You have protected your wife from this stressful situation by not telling her that you are no longer employed by the company. You have been drinking more than usual as a means of relieving the stress.

EXERCISE 5 *The Man's Objective*: You are still in love with your former wife although you have continued your affair with your secretary, Marilyn. You have continued the affair partly out of loneliness and partly because you have found no easy way to break off the affair. Now, in retrospect, you wish that the affair had never begun and you had never hurt your wife so grievously. You wish that you and your former wife were still together.

EXERCISE 6

The Husband's Objective: You are not directly involved in the crime; however, you knew that the crime would be committed, condoned it, and were to benefit from the crime. You love your wife and children very much; you don't want them to know that you have any connection with the crime. The trial is about to begin, and it's very important for you to have the support of your wife and children during this crucial event. Your wife's presence in the courtroom and the support of your children will help in making the jury see you as guiltless.

EXERCISE 7

The Young Man's Objective: Furiously angry and deeply disappointed, you no longer care that she doesn't want to marry you. Her actions reveal to you that she is shallow and unworthy. In your opinion, you are glad that you discovered these qualities in her before the marriage took place. Nonetheless, you are consumed with a need to tell her off and let her know what you think of her value system.

EXERCISE 8

The Kidnapper's Objective: You are waiting for the telephone call from your confederate. As soon as your "buddy" calls, you will be able to release the girl. By that time your confederate should have obtained the ransom money from the girl's parents. The director will say "ring" if there is a telephone call from the confederate and then will represent the confederate in any ensuing conversation. If you do not get a call from your confederate, perhaps because he's been captured, then you must decide what to do with the girl.

EXERCISE 9

The Professor's Objective: You are embittered, trapped in a small college on the East coast where you teach European literature. You are estranged from your wife and daughter whom you haven't seen for eighteen years. Your daughter lives with your wife on the West coast, and they both receive money from you each month as part of the separate maintenance settlement established by the court. Once you thought of yourself as an individual of enormous promise, but now you doubt that you will ever do a single meaningful thing with your life. You have met this girl student who has evinced a surprising amount of interest in you. After despairing of ever again establishing a meaningful relationship with anyone, you find yourself deeply interested in the girl. Experiencing mixed feelings of pleasure and fear, you have discovered sexual stirrings and an interest that you felt had long since disappeared forever. You have reached the point where you know that you must either drive the girl away or do something about your feelings for her.

EXERCISE 10 *The Young Man's Objective*: When you first started dating the young woman, it was because you felt that her financial and social position might be helpful to you. You saw your relationship with her as a means of furthering your own hopes for a successful, affluent life. There have been a number of girls in your life and, in honesty, in the past you have been promiscuous. When the girl disappeared you suddenly realized that you are truly in love with her and now have her best interests at heart. You want to deal with her honestly and in terms of what you now realize is a very real love for her.

EXERCISE 11 *The Young Man's Objective*: You have decided that your mother needs the kind of attention that your job and schooling do not permit. You have contracted a charitable organization who has agreed to take your mother into their institution. Within the next half-hour workers from the institution will be coming for your mother. You must inform your mother of your intention and prepare her for her new life.

EXERCISE 12 *The Boy's Objective*: Your day has been a complete failure; you have cut all four of today's classes. You have frittered away the entire day in the campus coffee shop. Your grades in this, your first year of college, are not nearly as good as they were in high school. You haven't accomplished much in the way of satisfactory social relationships either. Your conversations with acquaintances have seemed pointless and fraught with irritation. You have simply sat around the coffee shop bored, frustrated, and obsessed with the idea that your life is pointless, your aspirations futile, and your personal life bereft of love. Somehow, all of these frustrations have found no successful way of being expressed. Later in the day you went to rehearse a scene for drama class, but even this turned out badly and your acting partner left angrily. After several vain attempts to communicate with people you know, you wandered aimlessly around the campus. Caught up in your despairing mood, you did not notice how late it was until a half-hour ago when you telephoned your stepmother. Your primary objective is to give your stepmother a satisfactory reason for calling home so late and not coming home to dinner when expected. You are ashamed that your personal life and goals seem so meaningless and stupid. You are embarrassed and find it painful to expose your failures and limitations to your stepmother. You love her and want her and your father to think of you as a well-adjusted, happy, popular individual.

EXERCISE 13

The Mother's Objective: Her last lover left her two weeks ago. She has learned that she has leukemia. She is alone, frightened, unsure of what to do.

EXERCISE 14

The Husband's Objective: You feel estranged from your family and, somehow, you feel that much of this is due to your wife's influence on the children. Admittedly, you have not been at home nearly as much as you might wish. Your career as a physicist takes you away from home quite frequently. You feel that your wife embraces too many faddish ways of doing things that are not necessarily a good influence on your son and daughter. Just now, when you couldn't find a writing pen to complete a report, you went into your fifteen-year-old daughter's room to borrow one of her fountain pens. While looking for the pen you discover that your daughter has birth control pills in her room.

EXERCISE 15

The Husband's Objective: For months you have noticed that your wife seems troubled. She seems to fear having the child and reluctant to become a mother. You need to learn why your wife is troubled.

EXERCISE 16

The Husband's Objective: You want to celebrate the obtaining of this wonderful assignment which will change the lives of your wife and yourself. It is the opportunity of a lifetime.

EXERCISE 17 *The Husband's Objective*: You love your wife and children. Partly because of the failure of your first marriage, you do everything in your power to make a success of this second marriage. You are aware that this marriage is not a complete success, but you do love your wife. Unconsciously she has made you feel guilty: if it weren't for you and the children she could now be pursuing a successful career in show business. You are feeling depressed tonight and decided to stop in a bar that you occasionally frequent. There you had several drinks and met a girl, Inez. She made romantic overtures to you, and without quite knowing what happened you ended up at her apartment. This is the first time since your marriage that you have been with a woman other than your wife. It is now two in the morning, and you are arriving home. Your objectives will be determined during the improvisation.

EXERCISE 18 *The Doctor's Objective*: Unknown to your wife, you are being investigated by the American Medical Association for irregularities in your issuance of prescriptions and distribution of drugs. Some AMA members suspect that you may be using the drugs and may be impairing your effectiveness as a physician. You realize that your position in the medical profession is jeopardized and you must be cautious in your practice. You are profoundly concerned that your wife's addition may become known.

EXERCISE 19 *The Woman's Objective*: Tonight has been a particularly successful prayer meeting with several conversions achieved. You feel elated and filled with fervor. You are anxious to make amends with your brother for whom you feel much love. You look all over the house for him before you find him buried beneath the covers in his bed.

EXERCISE 20 *The Young Man's Objective:* Despondent, you went for a beer in a Lexington Avenue bar. While drinking your beer, you and another man fell into an interesting discussion. The two of you continued your talk while walking together through the park. Your new-found friend suggested you join him for a drink at his apartment. Agreeing, you continued your pleasant exchange of ideas over drinks at his apartment. A little intoxicated, you were surprised when the other man offered some money to you putting the bills down on the coffee table in front of you. He then made tentative sexual advances. Frightened and shocked at the sudden turn of events, you swung at your companion knocking him to the floor. Grabbing the money, you fled the apartment. After a little while, your panic subsiding, you collected your thoughts. You were ashamed of having taken the man's money. Moreover, you liked the man until you discovered his intent. Concerned about having possibly hurt him, you returned to his apartment to give him his money. You found the door ajar. Inside you discovered the man in the bathroom; he has slashed his wrists and committed suicide. Returning to your apartment, you are in shock.

EXERCISE 21

The Man's Objective: You have decided to leave your wife for this woman even though you know it will mean great financial hardship for the rest of your life and, worse, the probable loss of your children.

EXERCISE 22

The Man's Objective: You always felt embarrassed and a little unworthy in your success as a model. You truly felt that if your life was to have value you needed a different kind of success, one in which you could legitimately claim to be creative and an artist. Secretly, you worked on a novel into which you poured everything you knew. When the novel was completed you sent it to all the major publishers. It was rejected by them all. Crushed by the realization that you weren't the talent you thought, you had a nervous breakdown. You still love your wife and always will, but it occurs to you that your marriage is one that is inherently turbulent. You desire and revere your wife but for your own sanity feel that you should no longer try to live with her.

EXERCISE 23

The Man's Objective: You are facing the death penalty for

kidnapping a thirteen-year old girl. You are filled with remorse, enormous feelings of guilt, and the conviction that you will go to hell for your misdeeds. You can't understand how you could have done such a terrible thing since you have never had a record of violence or of hurting anyone except yourself during your blackout periods. You feel that you may be innocent, but you can't prove anything. Starved for the alcohol your body craves, your mind has difficulty functioning.

EXERCISE 24 *The Californian's Objective*: You apparently are in genuine mourning for your father's death. However, some weeks earlier you had purchased a very expensive Ferrari, illegally using corporate funds to pay for the car. You had used corporate funds once before to buy a condominium in France. While here in the mountains on a skiing holiday, your father has received a phone call from the company accountant and learned that you have embezzled corporate funds to pay for the Ferrari and the condominium. You have been your father's favorite son; he was heartbroken by your misconduct. Your father did not take any action but informed you that he is considering demoting you in the company so that funds would not be available to you and, more seriously, disinheriting you and leaving all his wealth to your brother. In desperation, you left your Kentucky friend at the ski lodge and followed your father out onto the ski slopes. In the unpatrolled area, when you had determined that you were alone, you pushed your father off a cliff, causing his death.

EXERCISE 25 *The College Student's Objective*: You have had three drinks at the party although you followed this up with a cup of coffee before heading home. Only nineteen, you are concerned that the police officer may cite you for drinking. To make things worse, just as the policeman comes up to the car, you realize that you have a six-pack of beer, unopened, sitting on the back seat of your automobile. You are concerned that the officer may think you've been drinking and cite you for this. Should this happen, you will most certainly lose your scholarship at the college which has very strict rules about student behavior in the college community. You come from a family with very limited economic means and the loss of your scholarship would result in your no longer being able to attend this college.

EXERCISE 26

The Younger Brother's Objective: For many months you have been embezzling a portion of the firm's funds for your own private purposes. You have justified this in your own mind since eventually the business will belong to you and your brother. Further, you don't really like this kind of business and would like to get into one of your own.

EXERCISE 27

The Young Boxer's Objective: You are definitely on your way to success in the fighting world. The sportswriters are beginning to take notice of you and, increasingly, you are commanding better matches and bigger money. Realistically, you know the time is coming when you must drop your brother as a manager; you know that you must secure a more knowledgeable man for the job.

EXERCISE 28

The Old Man's Objective: Years ago you knew this southwest part of the country well. This ranch belonged to your wife's folks. Your wife, Ellen, and you moved onto the ranch after the death of her parents. Always filled with wanderlust, you found it difficult to settle down, even though you loved Ellen. One night, while Ellen was asleep, you packed up a few belongings and hopped a freight train. Ever since then you've skipped all over the South and the West, working as a farm hand, oil driller, and more recently as a handyman. Now you've learned you've got leukemia and have only a few months to live. You have come back to the homestead fearful yet hoping that Ellen might take you back during these remaining months of your life. It was the middle of the night when you got here so you decided to hole up in the shed until morning. You plan to go over to the farmhouse to see Ellen later in the morning. Feeling the cold, you polished off a bottle of bourbon to keep you warm in the shed. As the action begins, you are still asleep when the boy enters.

EXERCISE 29

The Younger Brother's Objective: You are aware that your older brother lies and is irresponsible. You feel that your parents also know of your brother's character flaws but refuse to deal with them realistically. No one has wanted to confront the older brother and discuss his escapades. You believe that your older brother is heading for a mental breakdown and is very much in need of psychiatric help. All of these concerns about your older brother are complicated by your knowledge that your father has a heart condition and should not be burdened with worries.

EXERCISE 30 *Medic #1's Objective*: You became a medic because you are a pacifist who decided to serve your country in this way rather than as a conscientious objector. You are deeply concerned for all humanity. You feel that your medical colleague is an insensitive person, although you respect his knowledge, skill, and courage. You believe that his activities are entirely motivated by his plans to be a doctor for the monetary awards, power, and recognition that the career will give him.

EXERCISE 31 *The Producer's Objective*: You have a string of impressive credits and are known for your skillful blending of artistry with good commercial values. When you became interested in producing A LONELY PEACE, you found your usual sources of financing would not back the picture. You have a splendid script and believe the film could become a classic of sorts. When you couldn't raise the financing for the picture, you accepted money from an underworld syndicate in order to get the picture done. The underworld organization made only one proviso: You must use the young actor whom you are about to see in your office. Although you had misgivings about using the young actor, you compromised your views in order to get the picture done. Surprisingly, the young actor has revealed himself to be a fine talent and most cooperative individual. With three weeks of filming already completed, you have felt that the picture is going very well. Your good feelings were shattered today by a meeting with the syndicate's spokesman. Without explaining he has insisted that the young man must be withdrawn from the film. If you fail to comply, all financing for the picture will stop immediately and they also implied that you could suffer other difficulties as well. The syndicate representatives have assured you that they will reimburse you for the losses necessitated by re-shooting three weeks' work and that they will complete the financing of the movie. You find the situation heartbreaking inasmuch as you believe that A LONELY PEACE will be a financial and artistic success. Moreover, the young man is talented and someone you have come to respect.

EXERCISE 32

The Son's Objective: You must reveal to your father that you have changed your mind about a career. You have followed your father's footsteps in taking a pre-law course at the university because your father believes law to be an outstanding and lucrative career. Your real desire is to pursue a career in music with an emphasis on composing. You have always been a little afraid of your father who has a powerful personality and ingratiating ways. Somewhat retiring, you have found in your mother the love and understanding you need. In your heart you feel that your father is only interested in what you do so long as it makes him more important. Facing your father to reveal your desires and intentions takes all the courage you can muster.

EXERCISE 33

The Old Man's Objective: You were once wealthy, but unknown to your wife you have dribbled away your money in gambling. You have taken out a very expensive insurance policy with your wife as beneficiary. If you met with an "accident," your wife would make a lot of money. Consequently, you have decided to have yourself killed by an unknown assailant. You have brought a gun to the restaurant and plan to give it to the young man. It is your plan to have the young man kill you. You do not want to know when you will be killed, and the death must appear to be a murder so that your wife can collect the insurance. You are fearful of death but see that it is the only way that you can make amends to your wife for the foolish gambling and loss of the family's money.

EXERCISE 34

The Girl's Objective: There is more than skiing on your mind. You have lied to your mother for the first time in your life. You have fallen in love with a college boy, Robert. The boy, who is several years your senior, goes to a university several hundred miles away. You have planned to spend the weekend alone with him at a ski lodge. Although you are certain about your feelings for the boy, you have some misgivings about the way he feels. In order to appear more attractive to him, you have told Robert that you are two years older than your sixteen years. Not wishing to expose this lie, you have accepted his invitation to go skiing. You don't want to miss this weekend meeting for fear the boy will lose interest in you.

EXERCISE 35 *The Mother's Objective*: Your teenage daughter has been taken away from you by the law courts because you have a criminal record that you have carefully hidden from her. There is little likelihood that you will be able to live together in the near future. You savor every chance that you get to be with this daughter whom you love very much.

EXERCISE 36 *The First Student's Objective*: You were part of a group of young men who were initiating Ron into your fraternity. Since fraternities are forbidden on your campus, you do not wish the college authorities to know that initiation rites were taking place. Since you were very drunk during the hazing of the initiates, you remember little of what transpired during the rites. You are surprised to discover the second student, a fraternity brother, at the dean's office. You remember his disapproving of the hazing and, consequently, his condemnation of your actions and his leaving the initiation exercises early in the evening.

EXERCISE 37 *The Neophyte Actress's Objective*: You are very ambitious and plan a career as an actress. Your objectives are complicated by an overly possessive, willful mother and a director who claims he is in love with you. You realize that you have always permitted people to dominate your life and that both your mother and this director exercise an unhealthy influence on you. You have been dividing your attention between classes at college and your interest in theater arts. You feel that you must develop greater personal strengths and the ability to choose your own goals.

EXERCISE 38

The Businessman's Objective: You were once a high-placed Nazi who, towards the end of World War II, fled to one of the South American countries. Since then you have become a successful, respected member of your community. In a successful effort to hide your past, you have married a woman of the Jewish faith. Although you originally married her to help hide your past, your relationship to her over the years has evolved into one of profound love and respect.

EXERCISE 39

The Black Man's Objectives: You want to get your wife admitted to the hospital. Unexpectedly, your wife has gone into labor two weeks before the anticipated birth of the child. You had planned to be home in New York in time for the birth.

EXERCISE 40

The Wife's Objectives: You are concerned that the party be a success. Your husband has been drinking considerably during the past few months, and you are aware that he now has a serious drinking problem. A good social relationship with the guests is important since the husband is due for a major promotion within the large company in which he is a key executive. You realize that your husband's failure to get home at the proper time may be because he is drinking. You realize that his excessive drinking could be a manifestation of even greater problems: his need to succeed in a demanding and highly competitive business and his failure to have a wholly satisfactory marital relationship.

EXERCISE 41

The Driver's Objective: You are determined to get away from the accident as soon as possible. As driver of the car, you are in serious trouble. You were in a previous automobile accident in which it was proven that you were negligent. The judge informed you that, if you should have another accident, you would lose your license permanently.

EXERCISE 42

The Teacher's Objectives: You have failed the parent's boy, and he will have to stay back a year in the school. Admittedly, the boy failed a crucial test by only one point, but it is important to make the parent understand that some standards must prevail, even in a school where the children are emotionally disturbed.

EXERCISE 43 *The Person Entering the Room's Objective*: You have a sense of dread; you are convinced that something terrible is going to happen to you, but you haven't the slightest idea what it might be. The person who is already in the room is unknown to you but, for some irrational reason, seems dangerous to you. You desperately wish that you could recall any of the events that have taken place in the last few days, but you seem to be suffering from amnesia.

EXERCISE 44 *The Supervisor's Objectives*: As the action begins, you catch the inmate who is trying to escape from the home. Unknown to the inhabitants of the school, you spent the better part of your youth in such detention homes. Deal with the situation as you see fit.

EXERCISE 45 *Roommate #1's Objectives*: You have taken a new suit from a department store; at the time that you took the suit you did it simply for the thrill. It was not your intention to steal anything of value and you're embarrassed at having been involved in a theft and you have resolved to not take anything from a store again.

SECOND CHARACTER

EXERCISE 1

The Young Woman's Objective: You love the young man very much. You realize that he has guilt feelings associated with the accident that caused you so much pain. However, you do not blame him for the accident and, now that you are getting well, are anxious to marry him.

EXERCISE 2

The Mother's Objective: You love your son very much. However, you realize that there has been a long-time conflict between your second husband and your son. You want your son to return home but are fearful of what will happen to him living in such sordid surroundings. You are fearful that he may fall victim to the various pitfalls that beset today's youth: narcotics, venereal disease, sexual abuse, a sense of hopelessness, and a lack of purposefulness.

EXERCISE 3

The Brother's Objective: Since your family has not heard from your now-famous sister for over a year, you have come to this city to find out why she no longer cares about or shows any interest in your father and mother. You love your sister and cannot understand her indifference and neglect of your family. You have read in the fan magazines of her new-found volatile temper. Moreover, there have been rumors of pill taking and other strange behavior that do not seem consistent with the sister you remember and love.

EXERCISE 4

The Wife's Objective: It has always been your practice to separate your life with your husband from his business life. You have never called him at his office or visited him there. Since he is a major executive with a large corporation, you have always understood that there have been business meetings during the evening hours that sometimes cause him to come home late. His increased drinking, his failure to telephone you when he has late business meetings, and his recent irritability have led you to suspect that he may be seeing another woman. In any event, his behavior has changed radically and you realize that you must do something about it.

EXERCISE 5 *The Woman's Objective*: You are still in love with your former husband even though your pride required that you divorce him. Since then you have been very lonely. You have met another man, a widower with two children, who wants to marry you. While you do not really love this man, you like him very much. In considering marriage with him, it seems advisable to you for a number of reasons to give up custody of Wendy and let your ex-husband have the child.

EXERCISE 6 *The Wife's Objective*: You love your husband very much and are deeply concerned by the accusations made against him. In addition, you are alarmed at the psychological damage being done to your children who are being ridiculed and belittled at school and at play by the other children. Consequently, you have decided it as essential that you and the children move to another part of the country until your husband has been proven guiltless.

EXERCISE 7 *The Young Woman's Objectives*: Your boyfriend's disclosure that he has been in a mental institution terrifies you. It is not his admission of a mental breakdown that has filled you with fear but the knowledge of his illness coupled with your own family's history of mental illness. Several members of your family have been mentally ill. Naturally, it has been a relief to you to know that such mental aberration has bypassed you. Now the discovery that your fiance has been in an institution panics you. You believe that the children of such a marriage must be marred and subject to mental illness.

EXERCISE 8 *The Kidnapped Girl's Objective*: You think it's possible that the kidnapper's confederate will either fail to show up or call your capturer. It is your thought that if he got the money from your parents he might desert your kidnapper and keep the money for himself. Another possibility is that your parents will not put up the ransom money for you. Although your family is quite wealthy, it is your opinion that they don't love you; through the years their interests have always been totally focused on each other. With considerable justification you have felt neglected and unloved by them. You are very frightened, but you find it difficult to believe that your kidnapper is innately evil. You fear for your life and must try to find some way to help yourself.

EXERCISE 9

The Girl's Objectives: You are nineteen, bright, filled with a zest for life. You have lived all your life on the West coast. Unknown to the professor, you are the daughter he has not seen for many years. You have come east to try to understand a man who could for so many years evince so little interest in his own child. You have deliberately fostered a student-teacher relationship with him, which you know gives him pleasure. You suspect that your father, not knowing your identity, harbors romantic feelings for you. You are torn between pity for him and the need to hurt him.

EXERCISE 10

The Young Woman's Objective: You have been very much in love with this young man in spite of your parents' disapproval and the differences in your backgrounds. Now you have just come through a traumatic experience. You have discovered that you have contracted syphilis and have been undergoing medical treatment for it. Since this boy is the only person with whom you have ever had sexual relations, you can only conclude that he is the cause. You are emotionally shattered and profoundly hurt.

EXERCISE 11

The Mother's Objective: You have become increasingly frightened of the hostile world outside this tenement apartment. You only leave it to go to the corner liquor store for whisky. You are trying to keep your son from knowing that you occasionally hallucinate; you believe you are seeing horrific creatures who try to harm you. You feel safe with your son. You want to be protected from anything that is unfamiliar and thus frightening to you.

EXERCISE 12

The Stepmother's Objectives: You have noticed that your stepson has been depressed during the last few months. His stepparent for only a year and a half, you recognize that it has been a difficult period for him. You have known that in the past he has been a happy and well-adjusted boy. When he did not arrive home for dinner tonight you were quite concerned; you don't know why he stayed at school so long or what he was doing. This behavior is quite unusual for him; you feel that your husband's son may be reacting with disfavor toward you as the new parent in his life. Your primary objective is to find out why the young man has stayed at school so late at night without phoning you until a few minutes ago.

EXERCISE 13 *The Young Man's Objective*: He is working on an acting career in films and thus far has had several small roles in television while he continues studying at an actor's workshop. He has good reason to believe that he will ultimately enjoy a successful career as an actor. He does not expect his mother; he has tried to forget her and erase the emotional scars of his childhood.

EXERCISE 14 *The Wife's Objective*: You wish to preserve a marriage which, while not wholly satisfactory, has been one that has given you material comfort and status in the community. You love your husband, but know that he is more interested in his work as a physicist than he is in you or your children. Since he is frequently away on business trips, you have drifted into a casual affair with a much younger man who is a friend of your son's. This has led to your having many friends who are much younger than the friends you share with your husband. You believe it is important for him not to know of this aspect of your life.

EXERCISE 15 *The Wife's Objective*: You are uncertain of the prospective baby's parentage. Although you are very much in love with your husband, you have reason to believe that you were unfaithful to him at approximately the time the baby was conceived. The reason for your uncertainty is that you attended a party at which a number of entertainers were present and, under the influence of drugs, you may have had sexual relations. You specifically recall being attracted to a famous black entertainer with whom you became amorous. Under the influence of the drug, you are not sure of the extent of your relationship with the man, but you realize that he may be the father of your soon-to-be-born child. You know that you should make your husband aware of this possibility.

EXERCISE 16

The Wife's Objective: Unknown to your husband, you were married secretly to a famous South American revolutionary who was a Communist. The daughter of a conservative businessman, few people suspected your alliance with this famed revolutionary who died in an ambush. However, you know that some prominent South Americans are aware that you are the widow of this celebrated Communist. You have never told your husband of this alliance, and you know that his political views are diametrically opposed to those of your late husband. Now that your husband is going to hold a critical position at the top level of government intelligence, you know that the FBI will carefully investigate your past. They are certain to learn of your former marriage and, hence, your association with known Communists.

EXERCISE 17

The Wife's Objective: Your theatrical career before the marriage was not very successful; it was a low point in your career that you finally decided to marry your husband. Marriage and children have left you with a feeling of frustration often sensing that, if you had gone on with your career, perhaps you would now be most successful. Your marriage has not been a particularly happy one, nor has it been too unhappy; there have been no violent quarrels. This evening at 11 o'clock you received a telephone call. A man's voice informed you that your husband has been seeing a woman, that he has pictures of the encounter between the man and the woman, and that you should ask your husband about "Inez" when he gets home tonight. This is quite a shock to you. You feel that, whatever you husband has been or hasn't been, he has never been unfaithful. You feel that his possible indiscretion is your fault. Suddenly you realize that, while there have been no happy heights to your marriage, your husband has provided well for you and the children and has given you every consideration.

EXERCISE 18

The Wife's Objective: You need the drug even though your husband has been trying gradually to take you off morphine.

Now you feel sick and your system craves the narcotic. You must get your husband to write a prescription for the drug so you can obtain it at the mountain community pharmacy.

EXERCISE 19 *The Boy's Objective*: You feel possessed by two spirits: a potential messiah and a potential devil both vying for your soul. Frightened by your sister's admonition that you may not be saved, you have gone to bed to escape into the warm, womb-like covers of the bed. You want to cleanse yourself of evil thinking and of the love-hate relationship you feel for your sister. Sometimes in your dreams you see your sister as your wife-to-be and this terrifies you. In going to bed it is your intention to be reborn as the messiah.

EXERCISE 20 *The Young Woman's Objective*: You are bone tired when you return home after a long day of study and work. It only takes a moment for you to realize that your boyfriend is contemplating suicide.

EXERCISE 21 *The Woman's Objective*: You feel guilty for being a disruptive influence in a marriage. It never seemed possible to you that you would ever be the "other" woman in an illicit affair. You feel shabby and unworthy in the relationship. You genuinely love the man whom you perceive to be a fine person. You realize that he loves you but maintains the marriage for the sake of the children. You realize that you are not getting any younger and that you are in a relationship that does not have a promising future. You must decide now what to do about your love affair.

EXERCISE 22 *The Wife's Objective*: You still love your husband, but you cannot help but hate him part of the time. His need to be unique, a special kind of person in the world, seems no longer important to you. Now you want peace and a less turbulent life. You have found someone to marry who is less exciting, less vital, less ambitious than your husband. You believe that life with such a man, while it will be less exciting, might still bring you the peace you feel you need.

EXERCISE 23

The Woman's Objective: You are the mother of the young girl who was kidnapped by this terrible man. Furthermore, your daughter was raped and left so traumatized that she has had a total mental breakdown. At present the girl is almost a vegetable; she is incapable of shedding any light on this horrifying event. The police have asked you to help justice prevail by getting a confession from the prisoner. You believe the man to be the rapist-kidnapper and will do anything to get him to admit to the heinous crime.

EXERCISE 24

The Kentuckian's Objective: You are coming to your friend's room in the ski lodge. You know that he is pretending to be in mourning for his father. However, unknown to your friend, you had followed the two men when they went skiing. You were just about to catch up to them when, much to your amazement, you saw your friend push his father over a cliff. Shocked by this murder, you have not told either your friend or the authorities what you've seen. Now it has occurred to you that if you were to blackmail your friend you could leave the Kentucky coal mining town forever and live as grand a life as your friend. You are torn between the conflicting feelings of loyalty for your friend, justice for the murder, and the need to change your life from one of poverty to wealth.

EXERCISE 25

The Police Officer's Objective: Just twenty-eight, you are planning a career in criminology and hope eventually to become a detective. Along with your own ambitions, you are financing your younger brother's way through college. This is not easy since you receive relatively low pay as a young policeman. Moreover, you are concerned at present about your job. Your superiors have pointed out that your arrest record is not very large and it appears that you are too lenient with the drivers you find breaking the law. You have real reason to believe that your superiors will make "spot" checks to make sure you are handling your job conscientiously. These superiors are especially concerned that you be strict with the college students since this community's activities center primarily around the school. You have stopped the boy's car because you have noticed that the car has a faulty brake light. When you get up to the car you notice that there is a six-pack of beer, unopened, in the back seat of the automobile.

EXERCISE 26 *The Older Brother's Objective*: You weren't in any hurry to go home tonight since you and Mary have been fighting frequently. After drinking in several bars you decided to return to your family's place of business and do a little extra work. You are surprised to find your younger brother still working at 11 P.M. You wonder why he is working such late hours; it crosses your mind that he is in a unique position as handler of the company's finances.

EXERCISE 27 *The Older Brother's Objectives*: You are deeply proud of your younger brother's ascending fighting career. In a sense you are living through your brother's success since your own career came to a halt. You were a good boxer and could have been an important fighter. Unfortunately, at a crucial point in your career, you threw a bout to your opponent in return for a payoff from a crime syndicate. You took the money figuring that in future bouts you could make up for this one loss. However, after you lost that particular fight, the right matches never were offered again. Now representatives of the syndicate have come to you and told you that your younger brother must throw tonight's fight. If the young man loses the bout, there will be $50,000 in cash waiting for him at his home. If, on the contrary, he should win the fight, one of the two brothers will suffer an "accident" that will leave one of you permanently injured for life. In threatening you, the syndicate representatives have been careful not to reveal which of the two brothers will meet with the "accident."

EXERCISE 28 *The Teenage Boy's Objective*: Your father died a few months before your birth and your mother, Ellen, was forced to raise you single-handedly. Growing up on a ranch without a father, you learned at an early age how to help your mother run the small spread. It was hard work for a woman without a man and only a young son to help. There were hired hands, but their interest in the ranch was limited to what was required of them and their paycheck. You've been a good student in school who hopes to escape the drudgery of the ranch and become a writer. Now your life is in turmoil; your mother died after a heart attack four weeks ago. Because she worked hard all her life, the constant toil speeded her death. You don't know whether to sell the ranch or keep it. If you hurry to sell it, you will probably lose money. Suddenly, as young as you are, you have been forced into an adult world and the need to make adult decisions.

EXERCISE 29

The Older Brother's Objectives: You have often been involved in minor thefts and misdemeanors without your family's knowledge. When your misbehavior wasn't too serious, you would sometimes disclose these escapades to your younger brother. Recently you broke into a fellow student's storage locker at the fraternity and stole some valuables. Today the police called you for questioning; while no arrests were made, the suspicion does point toward you. You feel that it is simply a matter of time before you are arrested. You feel that you must leave the school and go to another part of the country. You have come to your family's house to get your clothes, record player, and the other properties you value. You are very short of cash.

EXERCISE 30

Medic #2's Objective: You are a practical person who deals realistically with your circumstances. You plan to be a doctor for several reasons: first, you are eminently well qualified to do so; secondly, you desire financial success, respect, and the recognition that are the rewards of becoming a doctor. You are profoundly fearful of the position in which you find yourself at the moment. From the looks of your fellow medic's wounds, it seems likely that his leg needs to be amputated. Furthermore, wounded as he is, it is highly improbable that he can work his way back with you to friendly territory. The enemy may find and kill you and your fellow medic.

EXERCISE 31

The Young Actor's Objective: Son of a well-known Eastern city businessman, you know that your father's business is a shield to hide his underworld connections. When the syndicate suggested that you should follow in your father's footsteps, you fled to Los Angeles. There you got interested in acting.

After studying drama, you were fortunate to secure an interview with a producer who gave you the leading role in his picture, A LONELY PEACE. You have completed three weeks of shooting; happily, the picture is going very well. Even though today's shooting was hectic, the rushes have shown you that you are a good actor doing an effective job.

EXERCISE 32 *The Father's Objectives*: You love your son greatly. You realize that your relationship to him has been something of a failure. Two factors contributed to this: your work as an attorney, which is very demanding, coupled along with your wife's possessiveness in relationship to the boy. You recognize in your son many of the same qualities you had when you were young. You fear that your son's aestheticism means that he may have many of the same kind of desires that you had when you were his age. At your son's age you questioned your own value system, career objectives, and sexual identity. You wanted a career as a musician but gave it up for what you perceived as the more masculine profession of law. Since then you have had mixed feelings about your profession, but mostly you find it stimulating and meaningful. You fear that your son's interests in the arts may result in years of heartbreak without reward. Furthermore, you fear that your son may be tempted to live outside society's accepted mores. You realize that this threat existed for you as a boy and that it may exist for your son.

EXERCISE 33 *The Young Man's Objective*: You have been in and out of many scrapes with the law and with members of your family and friends. You've been on probation and have spent a few months in jail. Still, you are not an unkind person and you long to climb out of the meanness and poverty of your environment and make something of your life. You have come to meet the old man because this person has suggested in a telephone conversation that your job as an "adventurer" for him would take less than a day and you would get $10,000 for it.

EXERCISE 34 *The Mother's Objective*: You are very close to your daughter. She has become the most important thing in your life since the death of your husband. Your daughter and you have always trusted and confided in each other. Recently, while cleaning your daughter's room, you found in the dresser drawer an invitation to her. It was sent by a boy named "Robert" asking her to join him for a weekend of skiing. You know that your daughter desires to go skiing not to be with her girlfriends but, instead, to be with this boy whom you do not know. You don't know how to handle this situation since your daughter will know that you opened a personal letter of hers if you discuss the situation. You have always respected your daughter's privacy; this letter opening was impulsive and not characteristic of you. If your daughter believes that you have read her letters, she will perhaps feel that she can no longer trust you. Your aim is to try to dissuade your daughter from going on the ski trip without revealing that you have read the letter. You are concerned for your daughter's happiness and feel she may experience a tawdry relationship that will hurt her.

EXERCISE 35

The Daughter's Objective: You desperately want to live and be with your mother. You cannot understand why she is indifferent to your need for a loving mother. You feel that your mother is indifferent and perhaps callous to your needs and feelings.

EXERCISE 36

The Second Student's Objective: You were appalled at the initiation of Ron and others carried out by the fraternity. The first student and some of the fraternity brothers were very drunk; their irresponsible and dehumanizing actions toward the initiates filled you with disgust. The last thing you saw before you left was the first student and his friends burying Ron in the sand up to his neck. The tide was out so there was no eminent danger to Ron. Now, in wake of the newspaper report that Ron has died, you surmise that the fraternity brothers abandoned Ron on the beach so that when the tide came in he drowned.

EXERCISE 37

The Mother's Objectives: You are very strong in your convictions and most anxious to guide your daughter into sensible pursuits. You are convinced that your daughter's talents, while considerable, are not sufficient to assure the girl of a successful career. Moreover, you are not at all certain that you approve of the kind of people who are involved in theatrical pursuits; it is your opinion that these people are unnecessarily bohemian and morally lax. You feel that your daughter's happiness will be realized if she obtains a college degree. You are willing to make whatever concessions are necessary to get your daughter to give up her enthusiasm for show business and to pursue more realistic goals.

EXERCISE 38 *The Wife's Objective*: Although you are Jewish and your husband is a Catholic, you have been most happy in your marriage. You will make any objective choices on the basis of what transpires during the improvisation's action.

EXERCISE 39 *The Wife's Objectives*: You have gone into labor two weeks before the anticipated birth of your child. You had planned to be back in New York well before the expected date of birth. You must get admitted to the hospital. You are frightened, and it is obvious that the baby is almost due. Furthermore, you have never told your husband but you are pregnant by another man, a Caucasian.

EXERCISE 40 *The Husband's Objectives*: You are a key executive at the point in your career when you will either be promoted to the top echelon of the company or be stalled in your present position. The pressures of your work in a highly competitive business plus an unstable marriage have contributed to your drinking more than is good for you. You are at a critical point in your life; you think of yourself as a basically good man, and yet you find yourself compromising with your ideals and perverting the aspirations of your youth. In this state of mind, your belief in your own goodness has been brought to a test today. On your way home you have run down and killed a pedestrian. Unhappily, you were driving twenty miles over the speed limit and recall having at least four martinis. Getting out of the car, you discovered that the pedestrian is dead. You determined that no one had seen the accident and, realizing that you will be brought up on manslaughter charges if discovered, fled the scene of the accident. You are filled with remorse and fear.

EXERCISE 41

The Girlfriend of the Driver's Objectives: You want to do whatever is best for your boyfriend. You love him very much and sense that he is indifferent to you. You are most anxious to please and help him in any way possible.

EXERCISE 42

The Parent's Objectives: Because this teacher failed to pass your son by one point in a test, your son has committed suicide. You cannot understand how the teacher could have been so inconsiderate since, in his own quiet way, the child worshipped the teacher. You are emotionally crushed by the circumstances and filled with mixed feelings of anger, loss, and desperation. You need to know what motivated the teacher to do such a thing.

EXERCISE 43

The Other Person's Objectives: You are relieved and delighted to have someone join you in the room. Five days ago you descended the very same stairs and met someone in the room who was a stranger. You were suffering from amnesia and didn't have any idea why you were in this strange rooming house. The person who was already in the room was unable to supply you with an explanation as to why he was there. The two of you began to be friends when suddenly, while your back was turned, he vanished. Since then you have been alone. You have been surprised to discover that you never have a need to eat or drink even though you have been here for five days!

EXERCISE 44

The Juvenile Delinquent's Objectives: You rightfully hate nearly everyone. Your parents are separated; both have established romantic relationships that exclude you entirely. The school demands too much discipline; there is little freedom or consideration for the inmates as individuals. You feel that you are in a trap, unloved and always an outsider. You have no reason to care what the supervisor thinks since trying to escape the school will result in severe punishment.

EXERCISE 45

Roommate #2's Objectives: You have seen Roommate #1

showing off a new suit to others in the dormitory. Those sharing the dormitory have guessed that there is something wrong with your roommate and have spoken to you about it. You know that your roommate has not received any letters from home during the past week and you know that your roommate has been strapped for money. Consequently, you can only conclude that your roommate has again stolen other people's property. You are profoundly worried about what appears to be your roommate's kleptomania and you recognize, for your own good, that some action must be taken.

THIRD CHARACTER

EXERCISE 36

The Dean's Objective: (If you decide to participate) To learn if any college students were in some way involved in the death of Ron. You are concerned that unfavorable publicity could be very harmful to the school.

EXERCISE 37

The Director's Objectives: From the moment you met this young actress you knew that she had those special qualities that make for stardom. She is a unique personality. You are aware that it may be a very difficult task to get her career started, but once underway there are no limits to her potential. Moreover, you have found yourself falling in love with the young actress. While you do not believe in marriage, you would enjoy establishing an alliance with the actress for both romantic and professional reasons. You feel that, for her to be of any value to you, she must break away from her strong attachment to her mother. You hope to build the girl into a star. If this happens, it will boost your currently lagging reputation.

EXERCISE 38

The Unknown Man's Objective: You are a member of the Jewish underground whose orders are to capture the businessman, a former Nazi hiding in South America, and smuggle him out of the country and back to Israel to stand trial for his war crimes.

EXERCISE 39

The Nurse's Objectives: You don't know what the hospital's board of directors would think of admitting this wife of a black man. You believe that you could possibly lose your job over this incident. You have mixed feelings about intermarriage, and your family's personal experiences in this area have been a heartache. Your brother fell in love with a black woman, and when the community and your family couldn't accept these circumstances he left for the North; he has never returned, and none of you have seen him again.

EXERCISE 40

The Stranger's Objectives: You are a deputy sheriff. An hour ago you witnessed an erratic driver speed through an intersection, brakes screeching, and hit a lone pedestrian. You observed a man get out of the car, examine the dead body of the pedestrian, and after looking around and seeing no one get back into his car and leave the scene of the accident. You got the license of the car and have traced the hit-and-run driver to a wealthy suburb. Realizing that the hit-and-run driver is rich, you have decided to attempt blackmail. You have a small income from your job as a deputy sheriff, little prospects for the future, and this action can lead to a rosier financial future. You have decided not to report the cause of the accident if the hit-and-run driver will give you money to keep quiet.

EXERCISE 41 *The Male Passenger's objectives*: You are faced with a serious dilemma. Although an innocent party to the accident, you were in a previous escapade that makes you a questionable character. This accident may cause you serious trouble. You have been convicted for a robbery but because of your youth were placed on probation. You are on scholarship at the college. Your past, coupled with this foolish accident, could result in ruining your chances of completing your education and obtaining your life goals.

FOURTH CHARACTER

EXERCISE 41 *The Girl Passenger's Objectives*: You are determined that the poor injured person be helped. You are quite certain that he or she is seriously hurt and may die if help is not obtained quickly.

Name ______________________ Date ______________________

IMPROVISATION QUESTIONNAIRE

Following each improvisation you do, you should evaluate the value of the improvisation by answering the following questions:

1. Was I involved in the experience? Did I really believe in what I was experiencing?

ANSWER:

2. If I was not involved, what caused my estrangement?

ANSWER:

3. Did I censor? *Encircle one:* YES NO PARTLY
4. Did I edit? *Encircle one:* YES NO PARTLY
5. Was I free or inhibited? If so, why?

ANSWER:

6. Did I really see? Listen? Touch? Taste? Smell? In other words, were my sensory tasks fulfilled?

ANSWER:

7. As the improvisation progressed, did I find myself *more* or *less* involved?

ANSWER:

8. Did the audience influence my experience?

ANSWER:

9. Was I fully aware of my partner and my environment?
ANSWER:

10. Did I attempt to convey an emotion or did I allow myself to experience each moment without manipulation?
ANSWER:

11. Did I premediate? *Encircle one:* YES NO PARTLY
12. Was I "playwriting" instead of "being?" Did I allow my intuitions to guide my actions and choices?
ANSWER:

13. Have I experienced what it means to trust my partner and myself?
ANSWER:

14. Did I take chances or was I cautious?
ANSWER:

15. Was I honest?
ANSWER:

16. Did I surrender to the experience?
ANSWER:

Name ______________________ Date ______________________

IMPROVISATION QUESTIONNAIRE

Following each improvisation you do, you should evaluate the value of the improvisation by answering the following questions:

1. Was I involved in the experience? Did I really believe in what I was experiencing?

ANSWER:

2. If I was not involved, what caused my estrangement?

ANSWER:

3. Did I censor? *Encircle one:* YES NO PARTLY
4. Did I edit? *Encircle one:* YES NO PARTLY
5. Was I free or inhibited? If so, why?

ANSWER:

6. Did I really see? Listen? Touch? Taste? Smell? In other words, were my sensory tasks fulfilled?

ANSWER:

7. As the improvisation progressed, did I find myself *more* or *less* involved?

ANSWER:

8. Did the audience influence my experience?

ANSWER:

9. Was I fully aware of my partner and my environment?

ANSWER:

10. Did I attempt to convey an emotion or did I allow myself to experience each moment without manipulation?

ANSWER:

11. Did I premediate? *Encircle one:* YES NO PARTLY

12. Was I "playwriting" instead of "being?" Did I allow my intuitions to guide my actions and choices?

ANSWER:

13. Have I experienced what it means to trust my partner and myself?

ANSWER:

14. Did I take chances or was I cautious?

ANSWER:

15. Was I honest?

ANSWER:

16. Did I surrender to the experience?

ANSWER:

CHAPTER 6

DEVELOPING YOUR CHARACTERIZATION

There is no such things as a straight role; all roles require that the performer be a character actor. By this I don't mean that you must capture external characteristics and physical makeup that are divergent from yourself. You retain your own individuality, but you add to your portrayal those differences that make each role you undertake a unique character. You must employ emotional resources of your own that apply to the character created by the writer. Your characterization will be successful when it grows from a truthful use of your own inner resources while at the same time faithfully rendering the behavior patterns envisioned by the author.

In addition to concerning yourself with the inner characterization, you must develop the mannerisms and physical behavior that capture the external characteristics of the person. This outer characterization can frequently be illuminated in your acting by using material from your own life, from observation of others' lives, from characters you have found in literature, and even from your observation of animal behavior. In short, your outer characterization may come from every possible source.

Any role that does not include a real characterization will seem flat, monotonous, and static. Unfortunately, much of the acting we see on television fits this description. Part of this deficiency of rich characterization can be attributed to the frequently rushed filmmaking, but much of the poor acting lies in the limited imagination and skill of the performers.

Such actors have simply not learned their craft. These actors do not feel or know how to prepare a characterization; at best they can only adapt all roles to their personal appeal. Aside from the narcissism revealed by such actors, their performance inevitably becomes dull and uninteresting through repetition. This kind of "personality" acting was popular in the thirties but has partially waned as audiences have become more sophisticated. Moreover, such actors fail to do sufficient thinking about the script before the rehearsal. The consequent result is that they are at sea during rehearsal using this valuable time to experiment randomly instead of with a specific purpose that will lead them to the center of the character. By all means rehearsal should be a time to experiment, but your character's development will be much more focused and more rewarding if you have worked outside of rehearsal time. From the moment you receive the script you should begin to live with your part. Inevitably rehearsals are far more rewarding when the actor has done as much preparation as possible on his own. Then the rehearsal will avoid time wasted on irrelevant impulses and unfocused experimentation. Instead you will be able to use this valuable time to find the appropriate physicalization necessary to illuminate the inner life of your character and you will be able to develop more profound interaction between your character and the other characters in the script. Among those things you can do on your own outside rehearsals with the other actors and director are to explore the ways that your character may walk and move and the way that your character talks and uses sounds. By sounds we mean the groans, moan, snorts, throat clearings, and myriad sounds other than words that are natural to humans. No doubt many of these explorations will be discarded, but some will open aspects of the character to you and then you can bring them to rehearsal to test them in the interaction between you and the other characters.

Part of this work in a role which the actor does during the time preceding and following the rehearsal must be done consciously and analytically. While it is sometimes believed that Constantin Stanislavsky, the Russian director-teacher whose theories have become identified as the "method," relied mostly on inspiration, in actuality he believed that careful and detailed exploration were essential to working out the most appropriate and truthful emotional states.

Obviously an actor cannot always find in his life approximations to the experiences of the character he must play. In such situations you must employ the "Magic If." By this we mean the actor employs his imagination to choose those "desires," those "fantasies" which are similar to those of the script's characters although the circumstances which prompted these "desires" or "fantasies" may have been entirely different. Stanislavsky thought that actors must believe in the possibility of events in their own life before they could believe in events onstage. He saw the value of transforming a character's aim into an actor's aim. You should ask yourself, "If I were the character in this situation, what would I do?" Providing the answer to the "Magic If" enables you to react to the unreal life onstage as if it were real.

There is a great difference between searching for, and choosing in yourself, emotions related to a part, and altering the part to suit your more facile resources. Some actors are convincing and compelling in many diverse roles; you can be sure that such actors have correct working methods and choose the correct inner resources and outer characteristics to bring to a role. Having found an occasion in your own life that is reasonably appropriate to what your character must experience, you probe all those factors surrounding the occasion to learn what triggered your experiencing. When did the event take place; does the time of the event have any relevance to what you experienced? Where did the event occur? Did the extreme cold result in a sullen, alienated, bitter kind of anger? Did the hot temperatures result in an excited, animated, volatile anger? Why did the emotional event occur? Did someone say or do something that made it happen? Precisely what happened and in what exact order did things occur that triggered your emotional experiencing? You probably cannot find exact parallels in your own experiences to the responses and actions of the writer's character. However, by looking for similar emotional experiencings in your own life you are brought to a closer understanding of what motivates your character and what makes your character take the actions he does. By finding parallel situations in your own life, you are likely to be much more specific and more likely to suggest originality in your responses rather than falling back on a clichē-ridden "dramatic" reaction. British actor Simon Callow says that you must locate the character in you. "Only then will the energy spring from within, instead of being externally applied; only then will you have renewed the umbilical connection between the character and the author. Then, indeed, you will feel almost irrelevant: a receptacle, a conduit, because the character will start to follow his own instincts and lead his own life, just as he did when he first came flowing out of the author's pen."

When you deal with the emotional behavior in a script, true understanding is the result of your finding correct parallels to your own experience. For example, we all have mostly in jest exclaimed at one time or another, "Oh! I could kill him!" Of course we didn't really mean it but the vocal exclamation came out of a "trigger" that is very close to what actually might make a person murder another person. The emotional response that resulted in a humorous exclamation, "I could kill him!" to the emotional response that actually results in murder is a difference of proportion rather than a difference of feeling.

Therefore in creating your character you look for incidents in your life that were similar. You re-create as many of the details that lead up to and through the incident as you can and then use the stimuli that triggered those emotional experiencings as they apply to what your character is experiencing.

Concentrating on the stimulus rather than the emotion will result in a more effective characterization. Another way of saying this is to look for the "trigger" that caused you to experience a specific emotion. No one in life searches for an emotional feeling—emotion is always the result of various kinds of stimuli. So actors should not work for the emotion itself, but instead for the stimuli that result in the emotions being experienced naturally and organically. When using memory of emotion, then, you should be concerned with the stimulus: what it makes you want to do and what it makes you feel. Therefore, an actor attempts to avoid vague memories surrounding an event and instead looks for the exact conditions of environment, prior events, interactions between people that resulted in the desired emotion.

Thus, you can see that to become a superior actor you must immerse yourself into a role and be transformed by the demands of the character; you and the role become one. When you as an actor successfully make such use of characterization, you have earned the title of artist.

To create a rich, dimensional characterization, you must examine many aspects of the role. You will be able to describe the type of script in which you are appearing. For example, assuming the spirit of a script is comedic, you should be able to recognize that different points of view are inherent in characterization depending on whether you are playing in a farce, comedy, or comedy of manners. Certainly your characterization should be different in tenor if you are playing in melodrama than if you are playing in tragedy.

At the inception of rehearsals you should, preferably in league with the director, learn what is the "Spine" of the drama. "Spine" is a term that can be approximated to the backbone of the script. Stanislavsky in his "method' ' called it the "Super-Objective" and "Through Line of Actions." The "Super-Objective" was the main idea of the final goal of each performance. It can be identified as the primary thrust that propels the action of the drama forward from beginning to conclusion. The "Through Line of Actions" is the logical mental line running through a role and the script which you as an actor must be able to trace in your mind.

You must keep in your mind that whatever you do in a role must help to disclose the "Spine" of the script. Every detail should contribute to the atmosphere of the script. For you to effectively build a character, you must establish the character's relationship with the surrounding world and the character's attitude toward every fact and event.

Broadway director Harold Clurman said that his "Spine" for Eugene O'Neill's DESIRE UNDER THE ELMS was "to possess the farm." Every character within the play in one way or another was effected by this "Super-Objective," and their individual objectives were determined by the "Spine" of the play. In O'Neill's LONG DAY'S JOURNEY INTO NIGHT, Clurman said the "Spine" of the play was "to probe within oneself for the lost 'something.'" He pointed out that all the major characters were searching for "the true self which has somehow been lost." Mary says, "If I could only find the faith I lost so I could pray again." Later she says, "What is it I'm looking for? I know it's something I've lost." All of the characters feel an overwhelming sense of loneliness and a feeling that he or she is alone with his or her own secret and guilt. They adhere to the "Spine" of the play in their need for self-examination, a search into oneself and into others. They keep hoping that through understanding they will find forgiveness, relief, the connection of love which may overcome their loneliness and sense of loss. In your acting then, you must identify the "Through Line of Actions" which is the movement of the inner life of your character and through this the "Spine" of the play is made clear to the audience. For example, all of the "Through Lines of Actions" by Willy Loman in Arthur Miller's DEATH OF A SALESMAN lead to the "Super-Objective" or "Spine" of winning back Biff's love.

You should be able to state in one sentence the theme of the play. In Miller's DEATH OF A SALESMAN, I believe the theme is that man's quest for material success and status bankrupts his moral and ethical values and leaves him bereft of a sense of his own worth. You should recognize what is the turning point of the script whether you are or are not involved in that part of the material. If you are appearing in a script set in a different time period, you should familiarize yourself with the socio-economic-cultural factors that prevailed at that time; you should develop an understanding of that period's folkways and mores. Developing a background in the period may include reading historical matter, studying paintings or pictures of that period, reading novels reflective of those times. Finally and most importantly, you must know what is your character's "objective." Objective can be defined as what the character wishes, wants, desires; it is the character's goal, aim, intent. All the character's objectives within a script merge into one overall objective, forming a logical and coherent stream.

In determining your character's objective, Constantin Stanislavsky suggested the following formula: "I want or I wish to do so and so . . . and then follows the verb expressing the desire, aim, the goal of the character." For example, Hamlet's objective is to avenge the death of his father.

You should be well aware of your character's objective for the entire role at the very outset. You then pursue your character's objective throughout the script. This may mean that your character enters into conflicts with someone or something that thwarts you in the attainment of your objective. Eventually you either overcome these obstacles or you are forced to adapt to these obstacles and hence change your objective or be defeated in the attempt to obtain your objective.

If your character does change his objective, then you must ask if that results in your having a new awareness of yourself or of the world around you. Ultimately, what makes Sophocles' OEDIPUS REX one of the great dramatic works of all time is its pivotal character's confrontation with his own hubris and then the discovery of his own humanity that results from his downfall.

Having determined what is your character's objective, Stanislavsky then suggests that you are concerned with the "Action" your character does to get his objective. This "Action"—the attempt to obtain your objective—is divided into "Activities." The "Activities" are the various means your character employs to get what your character wants. There are inner and outer "Obstacles" that your character will confront in seeking your objective. The inner obstacles may include self-doubt, conscience, recognition that your motives are impure, fear of failure. The outer obstacles are almost always caused by other people. For whatever reasons, these people do not want you to achieve your objectives. Either singly, or in group, they resist you as you strive to obtain your objective.

On a simple physical level, it is important that you determine how your character walks and stands. The state of your character's health will be significant in how you determine to reveal his vigor. You may have certain facial and movement mannerisms that are unique. Such simple actions as the way you choose to cross your legs may tell the audience much about your character's economic and social status.

In a similar way, the voice you employ may tell us much about the character. Is your character's diction precise or slovenly? Is your voice pleasant to the ear or harsh and abrasive? Is your voice forceful or weak? Perhaps your character's voice is unconsciously loud, reflecting a lack of personal awareness. Does the rate of your character's speech suggest nervousness, or does it reflect slow wittedness? Perhaps the rate at which your character speaks may tell the audience that the character is erratic or conversely assured and demanding. Does the pitch of your character's voice suggest authority or lack of authority? Have you chosen to have such audible mannerisms as "stuttering?"

Even though there may be no direct allusions to your character's background, you must create a total life for your character. The character's family background must be determined: Are your character's parents alive or dead? Did you love them? Did you favor one parent over the other? Why? Did you have any brothers or sisters? Was there sibling rivalry? Are you married? Are there any children? If not, why? Moreover, you must know your character's social position. Does it make a difference to your character? Has your character's status been different at another period? How much education has your character had? What is your character's philosophy of life? Is your character's economic status related to your character's social status?

Once this background has been determined, you must consider the psyche of your character. What sort of temperament do you have? What emotions do you express most often? Are you a highly structured person or are you easygoing? Are you flexible or rigid in your behavior and viewpoint? Are you life loving? What are your moral standards? Are these standards the result of heredity or environment? Or reaction against heredity and environment? Do your moral standards reflect personal strength or weakness or, simply, the standards of the times? Are you an aesthetic person? If so, how? What personality peculiarities do you have? For example, are you generous or selfish? Why? Are you compulsive in any way? Why? Are you self-effacing or self-aggrandizing? Why?

Congruent with determining your character's background and psyche, you must know what the attitude of the audience should be toward your character. Should they like your character or dislike your character? Should they admire the character you are playing, or should they have contempt for your character? Should the audience sympathize with your character?

To assist you in creating a believable living character true to the writer's intent, you must ask yourself what are the differences between your own way of thinking and the character's way of thinking. Such questioning will assist you as an actor in being true to the character's behavior and not simply adjusting the character to your own psychological makeup. Carrying this questioning further, you may ask yourself, "What is the nature of my will and inclinations as against those of the character I am playing?" The self-indulgent actor assumes that the character and the performer's behavior patterns are synonymous; the artist never makes this error.

Once you have been cast in a role and read the script, then you should write out the answers on paper to the questions asked in the Characterization Questionnaire on the following pages. This is a method that is most useful to the relatively inexperienced actor. Eventually you will not need to use such a characterization questionnaire in order to probe your character in all aspects; you will automatically do so. By knowing all the answers relevant to your character that appear in the questionnaire, you are certain to create a believable human being.

CHARACTERIZATION QUESTIONNAIRE

You have been cast in a show or scene. Where do you start? What do you do to create a believable, interesting characterization? Before you begin, answering the following questions will assist you in developing a rich, dimensional characterization.

IN TERMS OF YOUR CHARACTER:
How old are you? ____________
What nationality, race, creed are you? Does this have anything to do with specific traits that you might have?

Even though there may be no direct allusions to your character's background in the script, you must create a total life for your character. Your family background must be determined. Are your parents alive or dead? Do or did you love them? Did you favor one parent over the other? Why? Do you have any brothers or sisters? Is there or was there sibling rivalry? Are you married? Are there any children? If not, why?

What kind of family relationships do you have?

What kind of education have you had? Has it been beneficial?
How has it influenced your life?

What is your social level? Do you like the people with whom you associate? Do you like the places you go and the things you do? Are you satisfied with your social status?

What are your politics? Did you inherit your point of view or arrive at it through other influences? Have your political views changed over a period of time?

What are your prejudices?

What do you do for a living? Do you like your occupation? If you could, would you change it?

What is your financial level and situation?

Once this background has been determined, you may consider your character's psyche. What sort of temperament do you have? What emotions do you express most often? Are you a highly structured person or easygoing and relaxed? Are you flexible or rigid in your behavior and viewpoint? Are you life affirming or life negating? What are your moral standards? Are these standards the result of heredity or environment or reaction against heredity and environment? Do your moral standards reflect personal strength or weakness or, simply, the standards of the times and your peers? Are you an aesthetic person? If so, how? What personality peculiarities do you have? For example, are you generous or selfish? Why? Are you compulsive in any way? Are you self-effacing or self-aggrandizing? Why?

What experiences has your character had or not had that have deeply affected your life?

What are your character's tastes, opinions, vanities, fears, aims in life?

What deep-seated attitudes about things—in life and therefore in the scene—does your character have and express? How are these attitudes expressed?

What points of similarity are there between you, the actor, and the character you are playing?

When you know your character's background, psyche, and moral values, you will undoubtedly be truer in your intuitive responses to the moment. At this point you should be able to recognize the major action of your character. You should be able to state in one sentence what your character's objective is.

As the character, what is your objective? What do you *want* in the scene—from the other people involved, from yourself, from the situation?

CHAPTER 7

THE ENCOUNTER SESSION

Designed only for advanced actors who have been working together over an extended period of time, this exercise is related to the psychological marathons (sensitivity sessions) that have been developed at Esalen and other institutes that deal with human behavior. The premise is that a group of individuals have been brought together at a resort motel for a long weekend of marathon conversation and interaction. During this period they will divest themselves of their hostilities, fears, insecuritities, and innermost secrets. In a session akin to group therapy these people from all walks of life strip each other and themselves of their illusions. In this exercise, encounter means simply owning up to your own feelings and revealing your deepest here and now emotions, no matter how painful, how dangerous-seeming, or embarrassing. Hopefully, the people at the marathon are eventually able to free themselves of the need to hide their true feelings.

In this exercise the teacher-director assumes the role of the therapist who guides the session. He or she should participate only when needed and restrain himself from unnecessary intervention. Each actor is given a character who for some reason feels a need to attend the encounter session and some of the characters in the exercises are related (with their relationship established in the cast of characters). These actors should be apprised of their relationship to each other but no other information should be available to the group prior to the commencement of the exercise. Usually this exercise can be maintained for three to six hours with occasional ten minute breaks. During those breaks the actors must not lapse from their characterization.

Each of the characters involved in the improvisation of the marathon session is described on separate pages from each other so that the actors will remain ignorant of each other's objectives, motives, and innermost secrets. As the exercise begins, the people have been engaged in the marathon session for many hours; they are tired and their nerves are frayed. The actors must not concern themselves if there are extended periods of silence when the marathon session first begins; soon enough there will be considerable action. One line of dialog is given to a performer to begin the session and to stimulate interaction. The line, delivered by actor "*A*" to actor "*B*" is: "You're a hell of a milksop. Your wife's sleeping all over town and you do nothing about it!"

A maximum of fifteen actors should participate in the exercise. Physical space should be limited so that all participants are in close proximity to each other. Coffee should be readily available and the environment should approximate that of a living room suite at a resort motel. The encounter should commence from the moment the class convenes.

Those attending the encounter session are:

"A" — a man in his thirties or forties. Played by ____________________.

"B" — a man in his late thirties. Played by ____________________.
He is married to "C," played by ____________________.

"C" — a woman in her thirties. Played by ____________________.
You are married to "B," played by ____________________.

"D" — a man or woman of any age, played by ____________________.
You are a well-known writer and known by almost everyone at the encounter session.

"E" — a man or woman of any age, played by ____________________.

"F" — a woman in her thirties, played by ____________________.
You are married to "G," played by ____________________.

"G" — a man in his thirties, played by ____________________.
You are married to "F," played by ____________________.

"H" — a man in his thirties, played by ____________________.
You are married to "I," played by ____________________.

"I" — a woman in her thirties, played by ____________________.
You are married to "H," played by ____________________.

"J" — a man between 30 and 55, played by ____________________.

"K" — a young man, played by ____________________.
Your father, "L," played by ____________________,
has asked you to attend the encounter session with him.

"L" — a man in his forties-fifties, played by ____________________.
You are attending this encounter session with your son, "K," played by ____________________.

"M" — a teenage boy, played by ____________________.

"N" — a woman in her thirties, played by ____________________.

CHARACTER "A"

A man in his thirties or forties:
You are a used-car salesman who has been married twice, divorced twice. You loved your second wife very much and were shocked when she asked you for a divorce. She collects considerable alimony from you and, apparently, has no plans to remarry. You distrust marriage and think that most men are exploited in their marriages as much as you. Develop an entire life biography which you feel is in harmony with the above information.

CHARACTER "B"

A man in his late thirties:
You are five years older than your wife, "C" ____________. A successful businessman, you persuaded your wife to marry you even though she was reluctant to do so. She was fearful that her sexual appetites were such that she would not be faithful to you. Unfortunately, this fear was well-founded. You believe your wife is genuinely loving toward you in spite of her need for other men. You are acutely aware that your sexuality is not strong. Moreover, there are two children in the family whose well-being deserves your consideration. Develop for yourself a biographical background of this character's life that you feel is in harmony with the above information.

CHARACTER "C"

A woman in her thirties:
You love your husband, "B" ___________, and it is almost unbearable when you are unfaithful to him. Moreover, there are two children in the family whose well-being deserves your attention. You are compelled to prove yourself attractive over and over again with various men even though you have little or no emotional feeling for these men. Profoundly ashamed of your nymphomania, you have kept it hidden from the community and, in outer appearances, you epitomize respectability. It is a part of yourself that only your husband "B" ___________, and you have known about until this marathon session. Develop your biographical background of this character's life that you feel is in harmony with the above information.

CHARACTER "D"

A man or woman of any age:
You are a well-known writer who has achieved considerable critical and financial success. In spite of this you fear that your success will prove to be a fluke and that your purported talent as a writer will not sustain past the two novels you've already written. You consider your success an accidental stroke of luck and not something you truly deserve. Develop a biographical background of this character's life that you feel is in harmony with the above information.

CHARACTER "E"

A man or woman of any age:
It has occurred to you recently that you do not like yourself at all; you understand how you have become the kind of person you are but it doesn't help you much in attempting to change. You are searching for a new personality, a new way of dealing with yourself and with the people you like and would like to have like you. You are convinced that the real you is not likeable or attractive. Furthermore, you only will undertake close relationships with people whom you sort of recognize can do nothing for you and will ultimately harm you. Develop a biographical background of this character's life that you feel is in harmony with the above information.

CHARACTER "F"

A woman in her thirties:
You are married to "G" ____________. You met him in Europe where he was serving in the US Army and the two of you promptly fell in love. You came from a good Catholic family that disapproved of your relationship to the American. You were married in Europe and shortly afterwards joined your husband when he returned to civilian life in the United States. At first, you had an idyllic relationship but then your marriage began to disintegrate. Four years ago you fell in love with an American, Gary, and asked for a divorce. Your husband, "G" ____________, blocked it by terrifying legal threats. You were a foreigner new to the country, you had not known your legal rights, so you submitted to your husband's threats and stayed married to him. He told you that if you left him, he would have you sent back to your former country. Because that country was now a communist state and you knew your Catholic parents would strongly disapprove of divorce, you felt that you had no acceptable alternatives. Consequently, you have remained married to "G" ____________ and your romance with Gary stopped. Now you want "G" ____________ to know that you have spent four years as a bitter prisoner, motivated from day-to-day only by hatred for him. Often you wish he were dead. Develop a biographical background of this character's life that you feel is in harmony with the above information.

CHARACTER "G"

A man in his thirties:
You hopelessly love your wife, "F" ____________. You met her in Europe when you were serving in the US Army and the two of you promptly fell in love. You were married there and shortly after your return to the United States she joined you. At first the two of you had an idyllic relationship but then your marriage began to disintegrate. She is cold, frigid, and hostile. You want to stay married to her because it is inconceivable to you to live alone. The idea of being unmarried among all your married friends frightens you. You cannot bear the thought of being alone, of having to deal with life as a single person. When your wife, "F"____________, imagined she loved an American, Gary, you were astounded. This infatuation occurred two years after your marriage. You threatened to have "F"____________ deported and sent back to her country which is now one of the Communist satellite countries. You believe that this marriage, regardless of the bitterness involved, is better than no marriage. Further, you truly love your wife and hope that someday she will once again love you. Develop for yourself a biographical background of this character's life that you feel is in harmony with the above information.

CHARACTER "H"

A man in his thirties:
Your six-year-old son was born with Down's Syndrome. It was a searing, difficult period for both you and your wife but the two of you decided to keep your child rather than have it institutionalized. The child is quite retarded and daily becomes a greater burden. Your wife, however, loves the child greatly. So much of her time is spent with the child that you feel cheated in the marriage. Frequently you have wanted to kill the child and, on one occasion, almost did. Your wife does not know the violent feelings that you harbor within you nor does she know that the child will eventually destroy the love you have for her. You want to have another child, hopefully a normal one, but your wife will not allow herself to become pregnant. Develop a biographical background of this character's life that is in harmony with the above information.

CHARACTER "I"

A woman in her thirties:
Your six-year-old son was born with Down's Syndrome. Burdened with guilt, it seemed to you like God's retribution for the life you lived before you met your husband, "H" ___________. Unknown to him, you lived a life of promiscuity. From the day you fell in love with your husband you have been faithful to him. You profoundly regret your past life and have never let your husband know about the guilt feelings you harbor. You persuaded your husband to keep the child rather than have it institutionalized. The child is quite retarded and daily becomes a greater burden; you find the child demanding more and more of your time. You know that your marriage has been partly destroyed by the child and sometimes you feel that you should have permitted the child to be institutionalized. Furthermore, you live in fear of having another child, believing that God will once again punish you. You have not allowed yourself to become pregnant again. You love your husband and profoundly regret the sorrow you have brought him. Develop a biographical background of this character's life that you feel is in harmony with the above information.

CHARACTER "J"

A man between 30 and 55:
You are Vice-President of a large manufacturing company. You were promoted to this position because you have a firm grasp of the technical aspects of the company. In your new position, you are required to deal more with the personnel in your organization. Your superior has declared that you are alienating valuable subordinates in the company by your demands. On the other hand, you feel that the company treats its employees with kid gloves, that none of the company's personnel work as conscientiously and as hard as they might. You believe that most of the people in the company are not interested in doing a good job but are only interested in collecting their paychecks for as little effort as possible. You wonder if this is not true of most people in contemporary society. Develop for yourself a biographical background of this character's life that you feel is in harmony with the above information.

CHARACTER "K"

A young man:
Your father is a successful businessman who wraps himself up entirely in his business. During all the years of your childhood, he has rarely been home. You are artistic and creative, qualities which seem lost on your father who has rarely spoken or shown any enthusiasm for your interests. Your mother is a kind, gentle woman who has been overly-protective as you have been quick to realize. You know that it would take very little persuasion for her to smother you; some of the affection she has lavished on you seems to you a substitute for the father's failure to give her sufficient attention. Wise to psychoanalytic theory, for a time you've suspected that you might be homosexual. However, you have found a girl with whom you are truly happy and you have a good, meaningful relationship. Neither of you wish to be married since the marriages you have both witnessed in your respective families have been disasters. Since you believe your father imagines that you are homosexual, you decided to experiment with such activity to see if his notions were true. After one such encounter you came to the prompt realization that homosexuality was not of interest to you and you've been having a happy relationship with your girl ever since. Your father is attending this encounter session with you. He is "L" ____________ . Develop for yourself a biographical background of this character's life that you feel is in harmony with the above information.

CHARACTER "L"

A man in his forties-fifties:
You are a successful businessman heading a corporation that demands much of your time. You are on frequent business trips that take you away from your wife and your only son, "K" ____________. You love your wife although you must honestly state that your feelings for her have never been of a passionate nature. Unfortunately, you have failed to build a very meaningful relationship to your son. You recognize that this distance between you and the boy is mostly your fault; your inability to spend much time at home is one of the causes. You are attending this encounter session with your son because you have a real concern for his future. He is a most intelligent, promising young man. You fear whatever failings he has are due to your failure to be a good father. His youthful interests are very similar to the ones you had as a young man. Artistic and creative, your son has evinced no interest in the usual areas that interest young men; he has evinced no interest in sports, business, or the more prosaic pursuits of life that lead to security and a productive life. When you were his age you had plans to become a dancer; you had several successful professional engagements when you met a producer who felt you could build an important career as a dancer. You were delighted with his interest and under his aegis your career began to develop. Unfortunately, during a drunken party you had a rude awakening when this producer seduced you and you enjoyed the experience. This frightened you terribly and you resolved that the performing arts were not for a young man who wanted to live a normal life. Consequently, you left dancing and eventually became a most successful businessman. Now you see your son repeating the same pattern of life. With an overly protective mother and you as an absentee father it seems evident to you that your son is either homosexual or may very well become homosexual. You are not at all sure that anything can be done about it at this late date, but for his happiness you would like to do whatever you can to make his adult years good and productive ones. Develop a biographical background of this character's life that you feel is in harmony with the above information.

CHARACTER "M"

A teen-age boy:
Still in your late teens, you have tried to commit suicide. Your attempt to destroy yourself was precipitated when you were arrested for pushing marijuana and LSD. Your parents, entertainers, rushed home to assist you in your conflict with the law. Fortunately, you managed to conceal from your parents that you attempted suicide. They are both loving people who lavish more gifts than time on you since they are so busy with their careers. Furthermore, they have maintained their marriage for professional reasons but have not loved each other for several years. You believe that they have both established new romances. The other adults you have met seem hostile and authoritarian; most older people seem only interested in imposing their ideas on you. You are attending the encounter session at the insistence of the judge who presided at your trial. Your parents agreed that attending the session might be helpful to you. In addition to missing your parents' affection, you are concerned because you have never had sex and you are fearful of making the first move. You don't believe that it's possible in our society to have a meaningful relationship with another person. You are lonely and at sea in your relationships. Develop a biographical background of this character's life that you feel is in harmony with the above information.

CHARACTER "N"

A woman in her thirties:
At the moment your world has fallen apart in every way possible. You realize that much of your present predicament can be attributed to your past childhood and now your own reliving in some part of the experiences you had in your early years. Your father was a stern, unforgiving man who believed in corporal punishment. Frequently you were beaten badly by him while your mother, an ineffectual woman, stood by silently. Now, nightmarishly, you find yourself repeating the actions of your father. You have had your two children taken away from you by the court because they are victims of child abuse. As a result, your husband has left you. You are filled with remorse and guilt feelings. You believe that anyone would consider you a monster and you consider yourself a monster. You are at the encounter session because the Judge handling your child abuse case insisted you attend as a condition of your probation.

ABOUT THE AUTHOR

LESLIE ABBOTT has worked for the National Broadcasting Company, Desilu Studios, Pasadena Playhouse, ZIV Television, Foothill College, and Diablo Valley College. He received his education at the University of Pacific, University of Southern California, University of Shrivenham, University of London, and Stanford University. A former member of the famed Actors' Studio, the author has directed more than one hundred and fifty plays including the west-coast premieres of BLUES FOR MISTER CHARLIE, THE IMMORALIST, MAN WITH A GOLDEN ARM, ALL THE KING'S MEN, A CLEARING IN THE WOODS, and seven original plays and musicals with his own company, Abbott-Abrams Productions. In addition to being on the faculty at Diablo Valley College, Abbott is currently artistic director of TheatreFest.